Neale S. Godfrey's

ultimate kids' money book

Illustrated by
Randy Verougstraete

SCHOLASTIC INC.

New York Toronto London Auckland Sydney
Mexico City New Delhi Hong Kong Buenos Aires

To my children, Kyle and Rhett:

I listen to you. I learn from you. I trust you. I admire you.

But most of all I love you.

Mom

ISBN   0-439-40734-6

Copyright © 1998 by Children's Financial Network, Inc. All rights reserved. Published by Scholastic Inc., 557 Broadway, New York, NY 10012, by arrangement with Aladdin Paperbacks, Simon & Schuster Children's Publishing Division. SCHOLASTIC and associated logos are trademarks and/or registered trademarks of Scholastic Inc.

12 11 10 9 8 7 6 5 4 3 2 1   2 3 4 5 6 7/0

Printed in the U.S.A.   09

First Scholastic printing, October 2002

All photographs by Silver Burdett Ginn (SBG) unless otherwise noted.

3: bkgd. Texas A&M Early Childhood Development Center. 4: Erich Lessing/Art Resource, NY. 9: Amos Nachoum/Corbis Corporation. 10: bkgd. Superstock; l. E.R. Degginger/Color-Pic, Inc.; r. Phil Degginger/Color-Pic, Inc. 11: clockwise from t.l. American Numismatic Association/Tom Stack & Associates; Laurie Platt Winfrey, Inc.; The Granger Collection, New York; The Granger Collection, New York; The Granger Collection, New York; Lee Boltin/Boltin Picture Library; Laurie Platt Winfrey, Inc. 14:1. American Numismatic Association/Tom Stack & Associates; r. Giraudon/Art Resource, NY. 17: Laurie Platt Winfrey, Inc. 18: t. Matt Bradley/Tom Stack & Associates; b.l. Lee Boltin/Boltin Picture Library; b.r. American Numismatic Association/Tom Stack & Associates. 19: l., r. American Numismatic Association/Tom Stack & Associates. 20: American Numismatic Association/Tom Stack & Associates. 21: t., b. American Numismatic Association/Tom Stack & Associates. 46: Michael Rosenfeld/Tony Stone Images. 49: Michael Newman/PhotoEdit. 52: Vic Bider/Tony Stone Images. 70: Reuters/Corbis-Bettman. 80: t. © Carl Purcell/Photo Researchers, Inc. 82: t., m., b. Courtesy, Ben & Jerry's. 89: UPI/Corbis-Bettman. 91: t. © 1998 Al Stephenson/Woodfin Camp & Associates. 93: Winfield I. Parks/© National Geographic Image Collection. 101: t. Robert Brenner/PhotoEdit. 106-107: Denise DeLuise/First Image West, Inc. 111: top to bottom Bryan Peterson/The Stock Market; Jeremy Hardie/Tony Stone Images; © Phillip Hayson/Photo Researchers, Inc.; Peter Pearson/Tony Stone Images.

Cover: Background and piggy bank. PhotoDisc.

Author photo: Jeanne Strongin

Editorial assistance provided by Pubworks, Inc.

Book design by Rosanne Guararra and Lucille Chomowicz

The text for this book is set in 12-point ITC Officina Serif.

The illustrations are rendered in watercolor and ink.

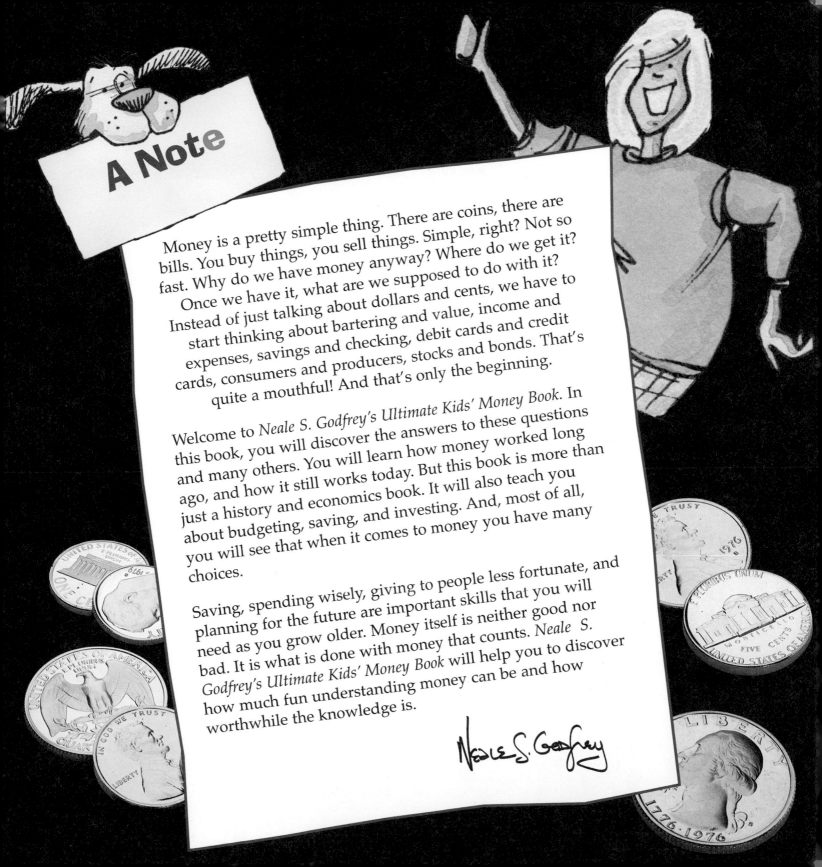

A Note

Money is a pretty simple thing. There are coins, there are bills. You buy things, you sell things. Simple, right? Not so fast. Why do we have money anyway? Where do we get it? Once we have it, what are we supposed to do with it? Instead of just talking about dollars and cents, we have to start thinking about bartering and value, income and expenses, savings and checking, debit cards and credit cards, consumers and producers, stocks and bonds. That's quite a mouthful! And that's only the beginning.

Welcome to *Neale S. Godfrey's Ultimate Kids' Money Book*. In this book, you will discover the answers to these questions and many others. You will learn how money worked long ago, and how it still works today. But this book is more than just a history and economics book. It will also teach you about budgeting, saving, and investing. And, most of all, you will see that when it comes to money you have many choices.

Saving, spending wisely, giving to people less fortunate, and planning for the future are important skills that you will need as you grow older. Money itself is neither good nor bad. It is what is done with money that counts. *Neale S. Godfrey's Ultimate Kids' Money Book* will help you to discover how much fun understanding money can be and how worthwhile the knowledge is.

Neale S. Godfrey

Contents

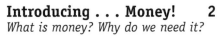

Chapter 1

Money—
Who Needs It?

We all do! **Why?**
It's part of our everyday **life**.
How did it all **start**?

Set your clock back 10,000 years. You're living in the days of the earliest people. You live in a cave or a shelter you built by yourself or with the help of your family. You eat whatever you are able to catch or find. You wear clothing made from animal skins. You have simple needs. You don't need much to survive. You certainly don't need money. After all, where would you spend it? There are no stores!

When did money come into the picture? Who invented it—and why? While we're on the subject, what is money, anyway?

You'll find the answers to these and many other questions in the pages that follow.

Money
It's a Necessity

Can you imagine life without **money**? How would you pay for food, clothing, and shelter? Could you go to the movies? Could you buy a CD? Without money, you probably wouldn't survive very well!

Money isn't everything. A lot of great things are free. You don't need money to see a full moon or a colorful sunrise. You don't need money to have friends. You don't even need money to have fun! But in today's world, you need enough money to get by, to satisfy some of your needs.

You need money to buy **goods**, such as food and clothing. You need money to pay for a place to live or to travel on a bus or a train. You need money to pay for **services** provided by doctors and dentists.

Think about it. You need money for just about everything.

A Penny for Your Thoughts

Is money always valuable? Suppose you were on a desert island. What good would a suitcase of money be? What would you rather have instead?

Word Bank

money *anything a group of people accept in exchange for goods and services*

goods *real items, such as cars, wristwatches, and clothing*

services *work that is done for other people*

2

. . . Money!

Everybody Pitches In

It takes more than an allowance and your family's money to buy all the goods and services you need to survive. Your town or city also spends money for your benefit. It pays for things, such as playgrounds and police protection. Even the government spends money on you by paying for things such as teachers, schools, and highways.

Where does the money for all this come from? These goods and services are paid for with taxes—money collected from people and businesses. No single person pays for such things alone. What other things are paid for by money collected by your town, city, or state?

Have you heard some of these names that people have given money?

bread, bucks, greenbacks, sawbucks, lucre, cash, ace, deuce, boodle, spondulicks, simoleons, shekels, mazuma, vishneggles, the ready, rhino, palm oil, long green, dinero, jack, cabbage, scratch, dough, lolly, oof, gelt, chips, beans, bits, berries, spot, bob, quid, yard, skins, lettuce

What a Deal!

It's a Long Story

What happened? How did we go from not having money to needing money for almost *everything*? One thing is for sure. It didn't happen overnight.

Thousands of years ago, people lived where they could find food. Groups of people often moved from place to place, looking for food. They would sometimes follow large herds of animals. Usually groups could not stay in one place too long because the food supply would run out.

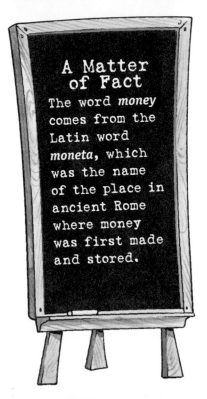

A Matter of Fact
The word *money* comes from the Latin word *moneta*, which was the name of the place in ancient Rome where money was first made and stored.

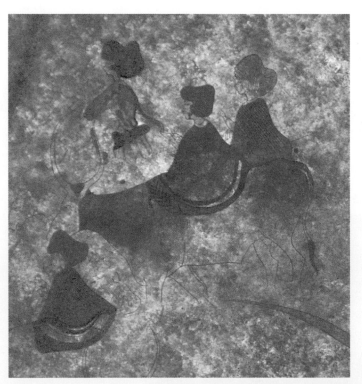

Cave painting of people on the move

Hello There, Stranger!

Though people moved around a lot, they still didn't see or know much about the world. They probably had no idea what was going on across the sea or beyond the next big mountain. There were no books, no newspapers, and no TVs. Imagine living then!

Sometimes, one group of people would meet another group and see new things—new things they wanted. Remember a time you saw something new you wanted? Groups might trade with one another. One group might trade animal skins for fish that the other group had just caught. This sort of trade made it easier for both groups to get what they needed or wanted.

Settling Down

Moving from place to place can be very difficult, especially when you have to move everything you own, including your home. Some people decided to stay in one place. They had to find new ways to get food. They started farming. They learned how to grow plants for food and raise farm animals. Now people could stay in one place and have all the food they needed!

Soon, individual farms grew into small towns, and small towns grew into larger ones. In these large towns, not everyone needed to help grow the food. There was more time to spend on other things. So people developed other skills or crafts. Along with farmers, there were now carpenters and blacksmiths, weavers and potters, bakers and butchers. What other types of skills do you think might have been needed?

A Penny for Your Thoughts

Suppose one day a month was a "no money" day. If you had to barter for everything you'd need on that day, what goods or services would you trade? What makes a fair trade?

Word Bank

barter *trading goods or services with someone for different goods or services, without using money*

To Market, to Market

Farmers and craftspeople couldn't use everything they made or grew so they began to trade goods. A loaf of bread might be traded for some cloth. Pottery could be traded for grain. A carpenter might repair a wagon in exchange for some tools. This kind of trading is called **bartering**. People traded things they had for things they wanted or needed.

But still, no money was involved. Money—the coins and bills we use to pay for goods and services—had not yet been invented!

5

Let's Go Swapping

Through bartering, people were able to get many things they needed and wanted. Merchants would sometimes travel to faraway places and bring back things made or grown in these places. People would then trade their local items for goods brought from far away. People, tribes, even different countries bartered with one another.

It's Still Going On

In some countries, people still barter instead of using money. Some countries even barter with each other. For example, countries that grow wheat can barter with countries that produce sugar. Kids barter all the time. Exchanging baseball cards, stickers, or snacks—it's all bartering.

Let's Make a Deal

Bartering was easy as long as there were only a few things to barter. People agreed on what could be traded for what. But when there were hundreds of items to swap, it got very complicated. If someone wanted a tent but only had three camels, he'd have to find someone who was willing to exchange a tent for three camels. Sometimes, people traded for something they didn't want in the hope they could later trade it for something they *did* want.

A Fair Trade?

Sometimes, people didn't agree on what things were worth. For example, how many monkeys should one barter for a canoe? How many coconuts? Which was worth more— monkeys or coconuts? What if the person with the canoe had other ideas? Plus, people had to carry around everything they wanted to barter with—and that got very difficult. Bartering got so complicated that people looked for an easier way to trade.

A Penny for Your Thoughts

In colonial times, people sometimes wanted to come to America but didn't have enough money for the boat fare. They would offer to work for seven years for anyone who would pay their way across the ocean. These workers were called indentured servants. Do you think they got a fair deal?

A Matter of Fact

Sometimes parents who wanted their daughter to marry a certain man would offer the man their daughter plus valuable goods, such as land or a cow. Sometimes it worked the other way around. A man had to give the woman's parents something valuable in order to be allowed to marry her. This still happens in some countries today.

In the Beginning . . .

It's About Value

Bartering became difficult because it was not easy figuring out and agreeing on the **value** of things. You can tell the value, or worth, of something by knowing what people are willing to give you in exchange for it. If someone were to give you two apples for one orange, the value of an orange would be equal to two apples. When people bartered, they needed to agree on the value of their possessions. Otherwise, they could not agree on a trade!

It's Common Cents

Instead of bartering or trading with each other, people sometimes used a medium of exchange. The **medium of exchange** was used as a common measure of value. For instance, if shells are the agreed-upon medium of exchange, the value of everything is measured in shells. Everything is paid for in shells. A hat may cost five shells, a pair of shoes may cost fifteen shells, and a coat may cost fifty shells. Whatever is bought is paid for in shells. With an agreed upon medium of exchange, buying and selling is a lot easier. Why do you think this is true?

A Matter of Fact
Many cultures used shells as money. The ancient Chinese used cowrie shells. Some Native Americans used wampum, which are small polished shells that are strung together.

cowrie shells

Word Bank

value *the worth of something as measured in goods, services, or a medium of exchange*

medium of exchange *anything that a group of people agree has a certain worth*

How do people decide how valuable something is?

It depends. If you were thirsty, the value of something to drink would increase.

Money, Money Everywhere

Different people around the world used different things for money. In many parts of the world, salt was used as a medium of exchange. Salt was valuable because it was needed to preserve and flavor food. It was also valuable because it was hard to find. Other items that have been used for money around the world include tea leaves, shells, feathers, barley, seeds, camels, dried fish, elephant tail bristles, and even dead rats! Just about anything you can think of has probably been tried as a medium of exchange.

Yap money stones

What's It Worth?

Unlike corn or salt or beads, most money has no value except as a medium of exchange. You can use a quarter to buy anything you want. Storekeepers use the quarters they get to buy anything they want. But the quarter has no other use except as a medium of exchange.

So why does our money work? It works because we all agree that it works. We agree that money has value. What if people decided that it didn't have value? Then our money wouldn't be worth a cent!

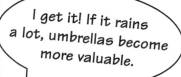

I get it! If it rains a lot, umbrellas become more valuable.

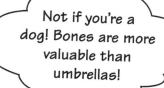

Not if you're a dog! Bones are more valuable than umbrellas!

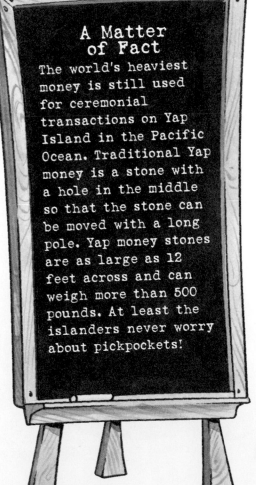

A Matter of Fact

The world's heaviest money is still used for ceremonial transactions on Yap Island in the Pacific Ocean. Traditional Yap money is a stone with a hole in the middle so that the stone can be moved with a long pole. Yap money stones are as large as 12 feet across and can weigh more than 500 pounds. At least the islanders never worry about pickpockets!

Coining Coins

Metal-ing in Money

But many mediums of exchange didn't work out so well. Feathers or seeds blew away. Barley spoiled. Camels were hard to move. Merchants needed a medium of exchange that was small, easy to handle and carry, and strong enough to last. They wanted something that people everywhere would accept in trade. They began to use **precious metals** as money.

Precious metals, like gold and silver, were hard to find. They were, therefore, valuable. Money made from these metals were accepted by many people because everybody wanted precious metals.

All That Glitters . . .

When people first decided that metal was the best material to use for money, they tended to use the metals found locally. These metals varied from place to place. Gold, silver, bronze, copper, and iron were the most common metals used, but lead and tin were also used.

Later, money made of gold and silver became the most valuable of all metal money. The people who used these metals weighed pieces of gold and silver to decide how much they were worth. Some early metal money was shaped into specially designed pellets or trinkets that were given a certain value.

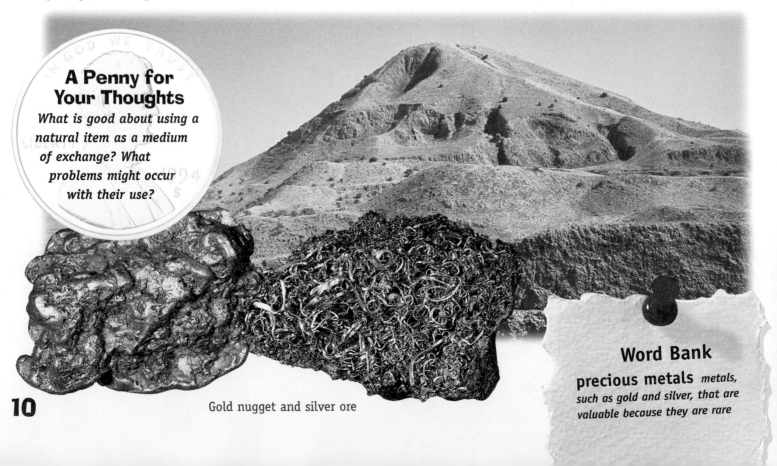

A Penny for Your Thoughts

What is good about using a natural item as a medium of exchange? What problems might occur with their use?

Gold nugget and silver ore

Word Bank
precious metals *metals, such as gold and silver, that are valuable because they are rare*

Penny and Greek obela

Early Greek money

The First Coins

No one knows for sure who the first people were to use coins. Some people think it was the Sumerians, an ancient people who lived in Mesopotamia (which is now part of Iraq and part of Syria) about 5,000 years ago. Others believe it was the people of Egypt, around 2500 B.C. These people melted and shaped silver into tiny bars. Each was then stamped with its weight and used as money.

By 700 B.C., each Greek city had its own distinct flat pieces of metal that were stamped with a picture or a design. These were the first true coins to be **minted**. By 500 B.C., coins were being used as money all over Greece and Rome.

Word Bank

mint *to stamp coins out of metal; a place where the coins of a country are made*

11

Gold!

In 640 B.C., Lydia, an ancient kingdom in what is Turkey today, used **electrum** to make its coins. Electrum is a natural mixture of gold and silver that is often found in rivers. To honor the king of Lydia, the coins were stamped with a lion's head. Lydia was the first country to use gold in its money. Gold coins eventually became the most valuable of all metal money.

Because pure gold is very soft, it is often mixed with other metals to make it harder. This mixture is called an **alloy**. The amount of gold in an alloy is measured in karats. One karat is 1/24 of the alloy.

Gold keeps its value because of its scarcity. There are estimated to be about 95 tons of gold in the world. That much gold would create a cube that measured 19 yards on each side!

Karats

- Pure gold is 24-karat gold.

- 14-karat gold is 14 parts gold and 10 parts of a mixture of silver and copper.

- 18-karat gold is 18 parts gold and 6 parts of a mixture of silver and copper.

Word Bank

electrum *a natural mixture of gold and silver*

alloy *a mixture of two or more metals*

Gold and other precious metals are weighed in pennyweights. Twenty pennyweights equal one troy ounce. One troy ounce is equal to 1/12 of a pound.

I thought there were 16 ounces in a pound!

Making Change

Coins became popular with people, and their use spread throughout the world. Pictures of great leaders were often stamped on the faces of the coins. Symbols of a country, such as birds, flowers, or animals, were also included on coins.

The coins were made of many metals—gold, silver, copper, iron, and bronze. Coins came in many shapes and sizes, but most were round. Countries were proud of their coins.

Before long, money as we know it was being used in trade throughout Europe, Asia, and the Middle East. Metal money made trade with other countries easier. Everything had an agreed-upon value, with money as the common medium of exchange. There were a few new complications because not all towns and countries used the same money. But it was much better than bartering.

But bartering did not disappear entirely. At first, money was used only by wealthy people for paying taxes. For many day-to-day things, people still bartered. Workers were often paid for their services with food, clothing, or a place to live. Even today, people still barter.

Metal Money— A Bestseller

Metal money was very popular for several reasons.

1. It was easy to carry—no matter where you went!
2. It didn't wear out easily.
3. There was a limited supply—it didn't grow on trees! But there was still enough so it wouldn't run out.
4. It could be changed when necessary. One coin could have one value stamped on it and another coin could have another value. Old money could also be melted down to make new money.

There are! But those ounces are called avoirdupois ounces. They're the ounces we use when we weigh most things.

I knew that!

Avoirdupois ounces! Troy ounces! No matter how you weigh it—a pound is still a pound!

13

Out With the Gold

Eureka!

About 2,000 years ago, the Chinese invented both paper and a printing process. They also invented paper money! China did not have a large enough supply of metals for making coins. Instead, they hit upon the idea of making money out of paper. Each paper note was guaranteed by the government to have a certain value. Paper money quickly became their medium of exchange!

Europe at that time was using only coins. So when the explorer Marco Polo returned to Italy from China in 1295, he brought back exciting news: China had been using paper money for hundreds of years! But Europeans couldn't understand how paper could be valuable. It took another 400 years before Europeans caught on and started making paper money of their own.

A Matter of Fact

Hundreds of years ago, money was kept in money boxes. Eventually the word for money box—*caisse* in French, *cassa* in Italian—became the English word *cash*.

Early Chinese paper money

Marco Polo

n With the New

Guard Your Gold!

By the time of the Middle Ages in Europe (A.D. 800–1100), gold had become a popular medium for trade. But gold was heavy and difficult to carry. As only kings had access to safes, people often carried all their money around with them. That was a particular problem for wealthy people. Besides, streets and roads were not safe. It was dangerous to carry large amounts of gold.

The legend of Robin Hood began and spread quickly in the Middle Ages. He and his followers lived in the forest, stealing gold from the rich to give to the poor. To prevent people from having to carry so much gold, merchants and goldsmiths started issuing notes, promising to pay gold to the person carrying the note. These **promissory notes** were the beginning of paper money in Europe.

Before Its Time

Still, people in Europe felt safer using coins. Gold and silver were precious metals that would never lose their value because they could always be melted down. In the Middle Ages, Europe was made up of many small states that were at constant war with one another. The people did not have enough confidence in their governments to trust paper money. In fact, it wasn't until 1661 that Sweden became the first European country to print money on paper.

A Penny for Your Thoughts
Coins are fairly easy to carry around, but if you have a lot of them, they can be very heavy! Paper money is much lighter to carry. It is also much cheaper to make than coins. What other benefits does paper money have over coins? What are the drawbacks?

Word Bank
promissory note *a written promise to pay a sum of money*

Take Your Pick!

Worth His Weight in Gold

In Greek mythology, King Midas wished that everything he touched would turn to gold. He made a big mistake! Everything he touched turned to gold, including his food! Today, when someone is successful at making a lot of money, we say he or she has the "Midas touch."

Read the story of Midas yourself. Find out what happens in the end. What do you think the phrase "All that glitters is not gold" means?

Penny Power

Take ten pennies and arrange them in a triangle like this. Moving only three pennies, make the triangle point in the opposite direction.

16

Coining Phrases

Here are some common expressions relating to money. What does each expression mean? Can you think of more expressions related to money?

- *a dime a dozen*
- *easy money*
- *pocket money*
- *penny-wise and pound-foolish*
- *the buck stops he*
- *break the bank*
- *rolling in dough*

Weighty Question

Which weighs more—a pound of feathers or a pound of gold? Are you sure?

Chapter 2

Money
in America

It's made of **metal**.
It's **made** of paper.
It has **value**.

What was the first U.S. money called?
What did it look like?
How are coins made?
Why does a dollar bill look the way it does?
Why do dimes, quarters, and half dollars have ridges?

You'll find the answers to these questions and more in this chapter. You'll learn why Americans used foreign coins for years. You'll learn why early American paper money was called greenbacks. You'll learn how long it takes a dollar bill to wear out—and you'll learn what all the special symbols on money mean. When you're done, you'll be heads (and tails) more money-wise than you were before!

17

Whose **Money** **Is** Whose?

In the 1500s and 1600s, long before our country was born, many European countries started colonies in North America. What money did the colonists use? They used money from the countries they came from: Spain, England, France, and Holland. Early colonists also used Native American wampum as money.

But the most widely used coins in the colonies were Spanish silver dollars, often called pieces of eight because they could be cut into eight pieces called bits. The word *bit* is from an Old English word meaning "piece or morsel." Today, some people still call a quarter "two bits." Until 1850, Spanish silver dollars were the most widely used coins in the world. Many countries even adopted these coins as their own **currency,** or official money.

Colonial Cash

Since there weren't enough coins in the British colonies, people started making their own money in the mid-1600s. They called their coins shillings (s), pence (p), and pounds (£) like the money used in England.

The first British colony to make coins was Massachusetts. The government of this colony minted threepence, sixpence, and shilling coins. One of the best-known coins was the Pine Tree Shilling. It was named after the design stamped on the head of the coin. Later, in 1690, the same colony started a bank and issued paper money in several **denominations,** from two shillings to five pounds.

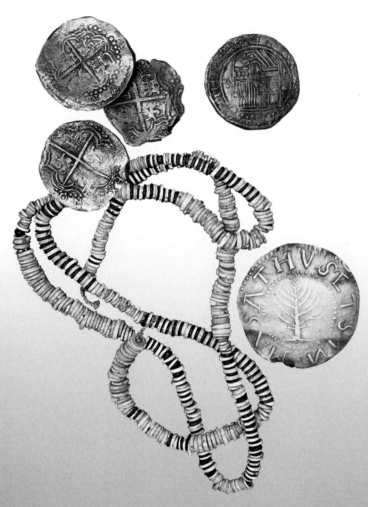

Early American money:
pieces of eight, wampum, pine tree shilling

Word Bank

currency *any kind of money that is used as a medium of exchange*

denomination *bills of a particular value*

18

Back When

War Is Expensive!

When the colonies declared their freedom, or independence, from England, a war called the American Revolution began. The war lasted from 1775 to 1783. As you can imagine, paying soldiers and giving them clothing, food, shelter, and guns cost a lot—a lot more than the government had on hand. So it printed paper money, or notes, called **continentals**. When the government started running out of money, it printed more and more! When you print too much money, though, its value goes down. By 1783 a whole barrel of continentals couldn't buy a piece of cheese! After that, the government didn't issue paper money until the 1860s.

Franklin cent and a continental

We Are Independent!

When the American Revolution ended, there were 13 different state currencies as well as foreign money in the new nation. So Congress decided that the states should all use the same currency. One of the first coins was minted in Connecticut in 1787. It showed 13 linked circles with one circle in the center with the words *United States* and *We are one*. Each circle represented one of the original 13 colonies.

In 1792, Congress passed a law establishing a new money system, with the dollar as the main unit of currency. The same law created the first national mint in Philadelphia, Pennsylvania. But why didn't the Americans just use the British system of pounds, shillings, and pence? Besides being the money system of the country the United States had just fought in a war, it was hard for the average person to understand. President Thomas Jefferson thought it would be easier for all Americans if our money was based on the decimal system. And that's what we still use today.

A dollar gets its name from the German word *Thaler*, which was a large silver coin made in the Austrian town of Joachimsthaler.

Dollar sure is easier to say!

Not for me it isn't!

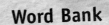

Word Bank

continental *paper money printed by Congress during the American Revolution*

19

American Money

Coins and More Coins

In 1793 newly minted cent and half-cent coins began rolling out of the Philadelphia Mint. Did you know that *cent* means $1/100$ of a unit, such as a dollar? Silver coins followed the next year, and gold coins the year after. The gold coins, called eagles, were produced until 1933. There were three different eagle coins, the $10.00 eagle, the $5.00 half eagle, and the $2.50 quarter eagle.

Even though America minted its own coins, foreign coins were still allowed to be used as money until 1857. But many Americans didn't like foreign currencies because there wasn't an agreed-upon value assigned to each coin. Imagine how difficult it would be to buy something if this were still true! Just try to buy those new sneakers you want with coins from ten different countries!

Early gold coins called "eagles"

A Penny for Your Thoughts

Suppose you could design a new coin. What would it be worth? What would it be made from? What would it look like? Whose picture would you put on it?

20

At Last!

Take Note!

After the government's experience with continentals, only banks and private companies issued paper money, or notes. These notes promised that the bank would exchange the notes for either gold or silver. All was well until some banks ran out of gold or silver to exchange for the notes. So in 1861 the U.S. government stepped in and printed the first official United States paper money. These notes were called **greenbacks**.

At one time or another in the United States, there has been a 1/2-cent coin, a 2-cent coin, a 3-cent coin, and a 20-cent coin! Now that's UNcommon cents!

Greenbacks

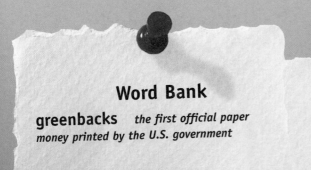

Word Bank

greenbacks *the first official paper money printed by the U.S. government*

What a Mess!

Even though the government was printing its own money, banks were still allowed to print notes as long as they kept some money with the government. But this led to confusion. Banks in different states, and even banks in the same town, issued notes, or bills. Sometimes banks issued notes worth as little as 3 cents; sometimes the notes were worth a lot more. By 1863 there were thousands of notes in existence, all from different banks!

In 1913 the government stopped letting private banks print their own notes. The government bought all existing notes from the banks and a new system was started. It was about time! The government began issuing all paper money. This was the start of the notes and coins we use today.

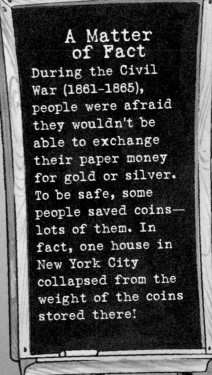

A Matter of Fact

During the Civil War (1861–1865), people were afraid they wouldn't be able to exchange their paper money for gold or silver. To be safe, some people saved coins—lots of them. In fact, one house in New York City collapsed from the weight of the coins stored there!

Coins Up Close

I understand calling the faces of coins heads, but where did the term tails come from?

Tails refers to the bottom or back of coins.

Cool Mints!

The coins we use today are produced in U.S. government mints located in Denver, Colorado, and Philadelphia, Pennsylvania. The mint in Philadelphia is the largest in the world. When it is not busy minting American coins, it makes coins for other countries. The U.S. Mint is very busy—it produces about 13 billion coins per year!

How can you tell where a coin was minted? Look at the head of a coin such as a quarter. The tiny letter to the right of George Washington's head is called the mint mark. It tells you where the coin was minted. *P* stands for Philadelphia; *D* stands for Denver. If you see an *O* or an *S*, that's because there were once mints in New Orleans and San Francisco.

Making Coins

Today's coins are not made of gold or silver. They are made from copper and nickel alloys, which are cheaper and more available than precious metals.

To make coins, the metal is melted and poured into molds to make bars, or **ingots**. Machines roll the ingots into sheets. Blanks for each type of coin are punched from the sheets. They are then put through an edge-rolling machine, which produces a raised rim. Finally, the designs on both sides of the coin are stamped at the same time. All United States coins have two sayings stamped on them: E Pluribus Unum (which is Latin for "Out of many, one"), and In God We Trust. The completed coins are loaded into machines that automatically count them and drop them into bags, which are weighed and sent off to banks.

Word Bank

ingot *metal cast in a convenient shape before it is made into something else*

22

Mill-ions of Coins

Find a dime or a quarter and run your finger around the edge. Feel the ridges. Coins haven't always had ridges. **Milled coins**, coins with ridges, were created to solve a problem. When coins were still made from gold and silver, some people would shave the edges of the coins and sell the valuable scraps. Ridges were put on the edges of the coins to stop this. Even though quarters and dimes are no longer made of silver, they still have ridges around the edges.

A Penny for Your Thoughts

By law, money cannot show a living person. This law was passed so that no person could mint coins as a sign of power, as the English kings did. Do you think this is still a good idea?

A Dollar That Thinks It's a Quarter

In 1979 the United States minted a new one-dollar coin. On it was a picture of Susan B. Anthony, who fought for women's rights in the late 1800s. The government thought people would prefer the convenience of a dollar coin. However, it was too much like a quarter in size, and people were easily confused. Millions of Susan B. Anthony dollars were minted, but only a small number were circulated. Now the government has 400 million of these coins in storage!

Word Bank

milled coins *coins with ridged edges*

Whose images are on the other sides of these coins?

1. penny
2. nickel
3. dime
4. quarter
5. half dollar

1. Abraham Lincoln; 2. Thomas Jefferson; 3. Franklin D. Roosevelt; 4. George Washington; 5. John F. Kennedy

The Paper Chase!

Pressing Issues

All paper money is printed at the Bureau of Engraving and Printing in Washington, D.C. That's where postage stamps are also printed. What do you think paper money is made from? If you said paper, you're wrong! It is made from a special blend of 25% cotton and 75% linen, which lasts longer. It is against the law to make this special blend without permission from the Bureau of Engraving and Printing. About 30 bills can be printed on a single sheet of paper. After the bills are printed, they are cut apart, pressed, starched, and bundled.

No Faking!

To stop people from making **counterfeit**, or fake, money, bills are made in a very particular way. Each bill has a serial number printed on it for identification. The serial numbers are recorded so the government knows exactly which bills are in circulation. There are different inks used to print bills, but only one company has the special secret formulas for making them. Also, even though you can't see them, there are red and blue fibers, or threads, running through each bill.

Word Bank

counterfeit   *to make a copy of something that people will think is genuine*

A Matter of Fact
To protect against counterfeiting, federal law says that any picture of American money must be printed either larger or smaller than it really is. The bills can be reproduced in color only if the picture is on one side.

Did you ever really take a good look at a dollar bill? Try it! What do you see?

1 This mark tells you which Federal Reserve Bank first issued the bill.

A Boston	E Richmond	I Minneapolis
B New York	F Atlanta	J Kansas City
C Philadelphia	G Chicago	K Dallas
D Cleveland	H St. Louis	L San Francisco

2 This is the serial number of the bill. Every bill has a different number.

3 This is the signature of the treasurer of the United States at the time the bill is printed.

4 This shows the date that this bill design was first used.

5 This is the great seal of the United States. The unfinished pyramid symbolizes growth. The eye represents the watchful gaze of God.

6 The eagle, the symbol of the United States, stands for strength. Thirteen stars and stripes stand for the first 13 states.

7 The olive branch stands for peace. The arrows show that Americans will fight to defend themselves.

25

Big Bucks!

The largest denomination of a bill ever printed in the United States was the $100,000 bill. Imagine making change for that! Actually, the $100,000 bill was used only to make payments between banks. For a while the Bureau of Engraving and Printing made $500; $1,000; $5,000; and $10,000 bills. Since very few people used them, they are no longer made. Today the largest bill in circulation is the $100 bill.

Do you know whose portraits belong on these bills?

Maybe someday my face will appear on a bill!

But you won't get to see it—you have to be dead to have your face on a coin or bill.

Keeping Count

The government keeps careful track of how much money is made and used. When paper money gets too old or worn, it's taken out of circulation. Then the money is shredded. It used to be burned, but this practice was stopped because of the pollution this caused. The average life of a dollar bill is 18 months, but a $50 bill lasts 9 years!

Every day the Bureau of Printing and Engraving receives thousands of bills that have been badly mangled or destroyed. Most of them are replaced with new bills. The Bureau has received money that had been stuffed in mattresses, chewed by mice, burned, and buried. It has even received money chewed by cows!

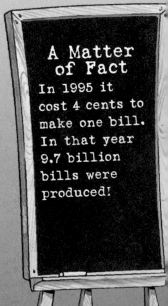

A Matter of Fact
In 1995 it cost 4 cents to make one bill. In that year 9.7 billion bills were produced!

$1–George Washington; $5–Abraham Lincoln; $10–Alexander Hamilton

Guarding the Gold

As you might remember reading, our dollars used to be backed by gold. That meant that you could bring paper money to a bank and exchange it for an equal amount of gold. This kind of money system is called a **gold standard**. But as the government got stronger, our currency did, too. There was no longer any need to back paper money with gold. In 1971 the United States officially abandoned the gold standard.

Without the gold standard the amount of money in circulation can be controlled without worrying about how much gold there is. However, the government still owns billions of dollars' worth of gold, stored at Fort Knox, Kentucky. The gold ingots stored there are locked inside concrete and steel vaults. The building is bombproof and is protected by many alarms and armed security guards. And it's never been broken into!

Around the World

As you learned earlier, the official unit of currency in the United States is the dollar. But most every country in the world has its own official unit of currency. In France the official currency is the franc, in Germany it is the mark, in Japan the yen, and in India the rupee. There are about 140 different currencies in use today around the world.

Most countries make their own money. Each country has its own special ink and paper. Each country has secret formulas and processes for coining and printing money. All the same coins and bills must match in size, weight, and appearance. Money all over the world is made very, *very* carefully.

A Penny for Your Thoughts

What problems do you think are caused by having so many different currencies around the world? Are there any advantages?

Word Bank

gold standard *the system of currency in which paper money can be exchanged for a fixed amount of gold*

27

Take Your Pick!

Make Your Moves

Rearrange the coins so that the pennies are in boxes 4 and 5 and the nickels are in boxes 1 and 2.

- You may slide a coin into an empty box.
- You may jump over a coin and land in an empty box.
- You may have only one coin in a box at a time.

Use real coins and a grid like the one shown. Can you make the switch in eight moves?

1	2	3	4	5

In Mint Condition

Naming Coins

Your friend has 5 coins. The average value of the coins is 11¢. What coins does your friend have?

On a typical day the United States Mint makes
451,000,000 pennies
2,000,000 nickels
10,000,000 dimes
4,000,000 quarters
120,000 half dollars . . .

That's a BIG pile of money! I wonder how much money (in dollars) the mint makes every day.

For that matter, how much money is that in 1 year? (If the mint is open 257 days per year?)

More than I can carry!

28

Chapter 3

It's **Your** **Money!**

What will **you** do with it?
How **can** you use
it **wisely**?

From beads to bank notes, money has changed a lot. Now that you know a little about the history of money, it's time to decide how to earn it, save it, spend it, and share it!

The easy part is spending it. You—along with all the other kids across America—spend billions of dollars a year. You buy food and drinks. You buy tapes and CDs. You buy clothing and movie tickets. You may even have a say in the food your family buys or the vacations you may take.

How do most people get their money?
What do they spend it on?
What's the best way to manage money?

In Chapter 3, you'll find the answers to these questions—and more. You'll pick up some shopping tips. You'll understand how to budget. In short, you'll be getting valuable ideas on how to get the most for your money.

29

Making Money

Do You
Yearn to Earn?

Have you ever heard the saying *Money doesn't grow on trees*? If the answer is yes, then you probably understand that you often need to earn the money that you spend. Any money that you earn or receive from someone else is called **income**. There are many different kinds of income. You can earn money doing a job such as watching pets, baby-sitting, or raking leaves. You can also earn money by keeping it in a bank. Even gifts of money from relatives count as income!

Word Bank

income *the money a person gets from salary or wages, interest, investments, and other sources*

wages *money paid to an employee for work done*

employee *a person who works for another in return for pay*

employer *a person or company for whom other people work for pay*

salary *a fixed amount of money paid regularly for work done*

Bringing Home
the Bacon

Do you have an income now? Some kids earn an allowance by doing chores, such as helping with the laundry, taking care of a pet, or cleaning up after meals. Some kids work outside their homes for extra cash. They may get paid money, or **wages**, from a business or a shopkeeper. But most kids your age like being in business for themselves. Have you ever had a lemonade stand or made something else to sell? If so, you've been a small-business owner.

Most adults get their money by working for it. People work for another person, a business, or the government. Or they run their own business. A person who works for someone else is called an **employee**. The person or company that an employee works for is an **employer**. An employer pays a **salary**, or a fixed sum of money, to its employees on a regular basis. Some people who are unable to earn enough income to survive receive help from the government to pay their bills. This kind of help is called welfare.

If you work for someone and you have somebody working for you, you are both an employee and an employer!

Even if you're a dog?

What's in a Job?

Plenty! Have you ever thought about the kind of job you'd like when you're an adult? As you can see in the chart below, some jobs require more schooling or special training than others. As a result, many workers in such jobs earn higher salaries. Do you see on the chart a job that you're interested in? Can you think of more jobs to add?

What would you like to be when you grow up? To help you decide, you might talk to people about their work. What skills do they have? How did their interests as a young person affect their job decisions? What special schooling or training was needed for them to become successful? What makes them want to go to work every day, besides the salary? Remember, it's important to enjoy the work you do.

Everything Changes

For hundreds—even thousands—of years, people have worked at different jobs. But jobs have changed over the years, and some have completely disappeared, such as lamplighter, iceman, and town crier. Other jobs have been modernized. For example, today's air-mail pilot has replaced the pony express rider. And some jobs didn't even exist twenty years ago! Below are some of the fastest-growing occupations in the United States today.

Fastest-growing Occupations

Health and medical field:	physicians, medical assistants, technicians
Computer science:	computer programmers, scientists, systems analysts
Human services:	social workers, child-care workers, chefs, cooks, gardeners
Travel:	flight attendants, travel agents
Teaching:	elementary school teachers, high school teachers

Job Training/Schooling and Salary

Job	Recommended Training/Schooling	Average Yearly Salary (1996)
Airline pilot	4 years of college and flight experience	$96,000
Auto mechanic	1 year of training	$24,000
Carpenter	3 to 4 years of training	$25,000
High school teacher	4 or 5 years of college	$36,000
Lawyer	4 years of college and 3 years of law school	$59,000
Physician	4 years of college and 4 years of medical school	$156,000

A Penny for Your Thoughts

Many jobs today couldn't have been imagined 100 years ago—even by science-fiction writers! Which jobs today do you think didn't exist 100 years ago? What do you think jobs in the future might be like?

Dollars and Sense

Have you bought an ice-cream cone lately? Some sports equipment? Have you phoned a friend or gone to the movies? If you answered yes to any of these, you are a **consumer**—someone who uses or consumes goods and services. A **producer**, on the other hand, is someone who makes goods or provides services. A producer may make the food you buy or serve you dinner at your favorite restaurant.

It's very easy to be a consumer. Anyone who has money to spend can be one. But it takes effort and know-how to be a smart consumer.

I grew my own vegetables and now I'm eating them. That makes me both a producer and a consumer.

Hello to "Good Buys"

Which of the following statements are true?
  A. *The size of a package tells you how much is inside.*
  B. *The more gadgets an appliance has, the better it will work.*
  C. *The best value is always a well-known brand.*

The above statements are all false! Are you surprised? Being a smart consumer is not always easy. It takes some work. One way to get the most for your dollar is to be a **comparison shopper**. That means you compare the different brands of a product as you shop. Read labels. Check ingredients. Look for the weight of the contents, not the size of the package. Compare prices and quality. Sometimes a product that costs more may be a better deal if it is made to last longer or comes with a better **warranty**. A warranty guarantees that the company that made the product—or the business that sold it—will fix or replace it if anything goes wrong, within a certain period of time.

Word Bank

consumer *someone who buys and uses goods and services*

producer *the person or business that provides goods and services*

comparison shopper *one who examines products to see how they are alike or different*

warranty *a written guarantee to repair or replace a product if something goes wrong within a limited period of time*

Does It Go?

The "Buy" Line

What costs hundreds of thousands of dollars, lasts 30 seconds, and is seen by millions of people? A TV commercial. Advertisers spend a lot of money "selling" products on TV. Ads can be useful to consumers. They can tell you about a product, a service, or a company. They can make you see something in a new way. But ads can also be misleading if you don't understand their purpose. They can make you want to buy or use something for the wrong reasons.

A Matter of Fact
On January 27, 1991, Super Bowl XXV was watched by over 120 million viewers. For a 30-second television commercial during that game, advertisers had to pay $800,000!

You have to sell a lot of stuff to meet those kinds of expenses!

Save, Spend, or Give?

When you have money, the first choice you need to make is whether or not to spend it. How much you save is up to you. How much you spend and how you spend it is also up to you. In general, people use money to buy the things they **need**, such as shoes or food, or **want**, such as a new soccer ball or computer game. But money can also be used for other things. For example, you might want to buy someone a present or **donate** money to a worthy cause or charity.

The choices people make about money are very personal. What's important to one person may not be as important to another. People have different ideas about needs and wants. To one family, having a car may be a necessity. To another, it may be viewed as a luxury. The key to being a smart consumer is knowing what's important to you—and why. What are the things you really couldn't live without? What things would be nice to have but are not necessary for your survival?

Word Bank

need *something that you must have*

want *something that you would like to have but don't necessarily need*

donate *to contribute money, a gift, or time to a worthy cause, fund, or charity*

33

Saving and Spending

The Ins and Outs of Managing Money

Where does your money go? That is one of the most important questions you have to ask yourself once you have money of your own to spend and save. Keeping track of how much you have and what you are spending it on—and knowing whether or not you can afford to buy what you want—are the secrets to success with money.

A **budget** can help you manage your money. A budget is a plan that shows how much money comes in and how much money goes out. Keeping a record of your income and spending can provide you with useful information. It can help you plan for the future. You might spot places you can cut spending in order to have more money for other things.

There are two parts to any budget.

Part 1: Money In

This part of your budget shows your income, or the money you get from your allowance, gifts, and jobs. Your income may vary from week to week.

Part 2: Money Out

This part of your budget shows how you use your money. It includes spending, savings, and if you choose, donating.

Spending includes everything you need to spend money on, such as bus fare or lunch. It covers those extras, too—the things you buy just because you want them, such as snacks or movie tickets.

Savings is money you put away to use later on. Savings can help you plan for buying things you know you will need or want in the future. Short-term savings is money saved to buy something in the near future, like a book. Medium-term savings is money you save over a longer period of time, probably to buy a more expensive item, like a bike. You also have to think about long-term savings, or money you save for the distant future, as for college. It could take you years to save for that!

I saved money by building a bookcase out of orange crates.

How clever! What will you do next?

Try to figure out a way to get rid of all those oranges!

Word Bank

budget *a plan of how much money a person, business, government, or organization has to spend and how it will be spent*

34

What's the Plan?

How It's Done

Look at Marta's weekly budget. What do you notice about how Marta manages money? If you noticed she doesn't spend more than she has, you'd be right. That's the sign of a good budget!

Managing money can be simple once you understand that what you have to spend is all you have to spend.

With empty pockets, I'm not going to be spending very much!

MARTA'S WEEKLY BUDGET

Money In

Income	
allowance	$7.00
gift from Uncle Joe	3.00
Total	$10.00

Money Out

Spending	
snack	$2.50
pen	.50
baseball cards	2.00
Savings (for bike)	$3.00
Sharing — UNICEF donation	$2.00
Total	$10.00

Get On Track

One good way to avoid running out of money is to have a weekly spending plan, like Marta's, and stick to it. The steps outlined below will help you.

- List all your income—all the money coming in.
- List all the things you spend money on regularly— for example, bus fare and snack. Include any new expense you expect during the week, such as a birthday present, and estimate the amount. That money is for "extras."
- Think about what you're saving for. Write the amount you need to put aside each week to make this happen.
- Finally, list any donations you might make to help others.
- Now you can subtract the *money out* from the *money in*. Your budget should balance.

35

All in the Family

Do you know where your family's income comes from? Do you know what your family spends money on? The chart below shows Marta's family's budget. It includes typical expenses for her family.

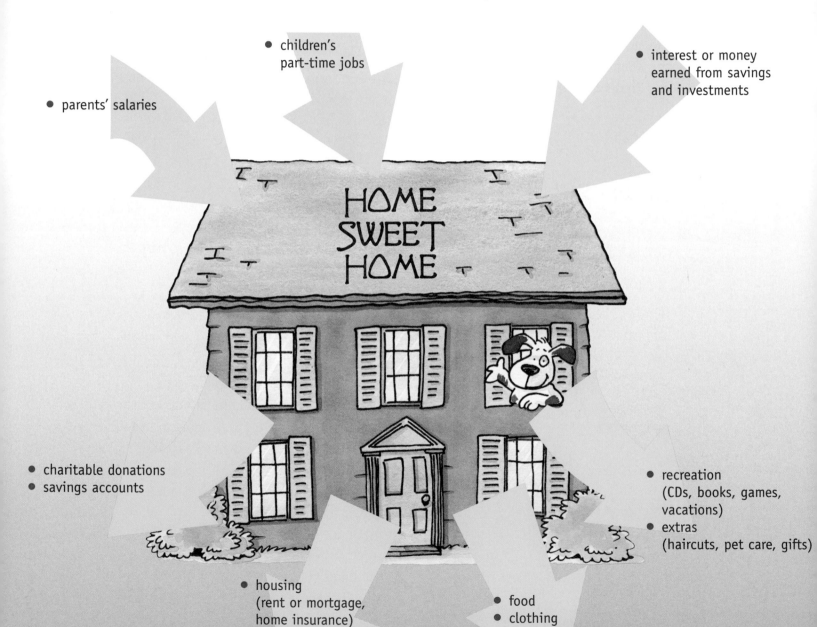

- children's part-time jobs
- interest or money earned from savings and investments
- parents' salaries

HOME SWEET HOME

- charitable donations
- savings accounts

- recreation (CDs, books, games, vacations)
- extras (haircuts, pet care, gifts)

- housing (rent or mortgage, home insurance)
- household expenses (telephone, electricity, heat)
- car payments and insurance
- taxes

- food
- clothing
- medical bills
- child care
- educational expenses

Budgeting—
It's All Around You!

So now that you know how to budget, you might be surprised to learn how many people are **balancing budgets**, or trying to make sure that the money going out is equal to or less than the money coming in. Not only do individuals and families budget, but businesses, organizations (like the Girl Scouts or UNICEF) and even governments budget, too. Wherever there's money, it has to be managed. And it should be managed wisely.

A Penny for Your Thoughts

What if your family decided to go on a weekend trip? Where would you go? What would you see and do? How much would it cost? Where would the money come from to pay for it? How could you cut costs?

Word Bank

balanced budget *a budget in which the money going out is equal to or less than the money taken in*

opportunity cost *the cost of what you are giving up to get something you want more*

It's a Choice!

One thing is for sure—budgeting involves making choices. You have to choose what to do with your money. How much should you save? How much should you spend? What should you spend it on? What are you willing to give up to get what you want? The cost of your decision is called an **opportunity cost**. The opportunity cost is what you are giving up. Suppose you want to buy a T-shirt and a CD, but you only have enough money to buy one item. If you decide to buy the CD, the opportunity cost, or what you are giving up, is the T-shirt. Can you think of some choices you've made lately? What did you give up to get what you wanted? Was it worth it?

So, What Do You Think?

Is spending as easy as you thought it was? It really takes a lot of work to spend wisely. You need to think about what you want today as well as what you want tomorrow.

37

Take Your Pick!

Time to Budget

Make up a monthly budget based on your allowance or on an allowance of $5 per week. How much would you save? How much would you spend? If you were saving up for a compact disc, how long do you think it would take you? What if you were saving up to buy a computer game?

Shop 'Til You Drop

Congratulations! You've just won a *million* dollars! How long would it take you to spend all that money if you shopped 24 hours a day and spent $200 every minute? What do you think you would buy (in one minute) for $200?

Mind Your Business!

If you need extra cash, you could start your own business. What product would you sell? Would you provide a service instead? Come up with a catchy slogan to sell your product or service. Maybe you could even write a little jingle!

Party!

You've come to the end of the chapter. Time to celebrate! Suppose you had $50 to spend on a party. Make a plan. Where will your party be? How many friends will you invite? What will you do? What will you eat? What will you buy with your $50?

Chapter 4

All About Banks

It's your **money**.
You **make** it.
You **spend** it.
You **save** it.

In this chapter, you'll find out all about banking—AND
learn how managing money can add up to big bucks!

Why are there banks? How old is banking?
How do I know if my money is safe in a bank?
How do banks make money?
What are some alternatives to banks?

These are just a few of the questions you'll
find answers to. By the end of this
chapter, you'll have a better understanding
of the statement *You can bank on it!*

Bank Notes, Facts

Banking: It's an Old Story

Banking is as old as money itself, dating back thousands of years. In ancient times, temples were the safest places to store precious metals. No one would steal from a temple for fear of making the gods angry. So temples became the first **banks**. There are records that date back 2,000 years, showing how much precious metal individuals had deposited in temples. Some temples even exchanged foreign coins and made **loans,** which let people borrow money with the promise to pay it back.

In ancient Greece, each city had its own coins. Traveling merchants paid money-changers a fee to exchange coins from one city for those from another. Money-changers also exchanged coins for gold or silver. The services money changers provided encouraged trade between different cities and foreign countries. Money-changers became the first bankers. Later in history, goldsmiths acted as bankers by keeping people's valuable possessions in their vaults.

A Matter of Fact

Early Italian bankers often conducted their business on street benches. The English word *bank* comes from the Italian word *banca,* which means "bench."

The first U.S. bank was established in 1791.

Wow! That was even before my great-great-great-grandmother was born!

Word Bank

bank *a business that keeps money for customers, makes loans, and provides other money-related services*

loan *a sum of money borrowed for a certain amount of time*

40

and Figures

Interest on loan 10%

Banks: Minding Your—and Their— Own Business!

Besides being a safe place to keep money, a bank is also a business. Like any other business, a bank needs to make a **profit**. Profit is the money left after a business pays its expenses. Banks make money by charging their customers for the services they provide.

Banks also make money by lending money. When you **deposit** your money in a bank, you are letting the bank use it. The bank combines your money with other depositors' money to make loans. In return for using your money, the bank pays you **interest**. The bank can then lend your money to someone who wants to borrow it. The borrower has to pay interest to the bank. But the borrower pays the bank more interest than the bank pays you. So the bank makes a profit by being the go-between—just like the money-changers in the old days.

Interest on savings 5%

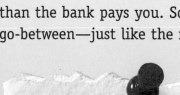

Word Bank

profit the money left over after expenses are paid

deposit the money put in a bank account

interest the money you pay to borrow money, or the money a bank pays you for using your money

Simply Interest-ing!

How does interest work? Suppose you put $100 in the bank and the bank agrees to pay you 5% interest per year. This means that the bank will pay you 5¢ per dollar every year. At the end of the first year, you will have earned $5. How much money would you have? What if you put $1,000 in the bank for one year at the same interest rate?

The Golden Rules

- Banks must insure their customers' deposits.
- Banks must keep a percentage of their deposits in a Federal Reserve bank.
- Banks must tell customers the interest rate on a loan.
- All agreements that bank customers sign must be written in plain English so that the customer understands exactly what it is he or she is signing.
- Banks may not make loans unless they are sure the loans will be repaid.
- Banks may not discriminate against anyone on account of age, sex, religion, race, or ethnic background.

The Loan Ranger

Are banks allowed to lend all of their money? No, of course not! The Federal Reserve System, the central bank of the United States, makes sure banks take good care of your money. The "Fed" requires that banks keep a certain percentage of their deposits on hand or in a Federal Reserve bank. That way, when people want their money back, they can get it.

A Penny for Your Thoughts

Government laws limit the interest that banks may charge for loans. What do you think would happen if there were no such laws? Do you think all banks charge the same rates? Are these laws good for the customer?

Keeping Track of
Business

How do banks keep track of everyone's money? By keeping accurate records of every **transaction** in each customer's account. Customers fill out slips of paper for every deposit or **withdrawal**. They get a receipt from the bank, which is proof of the transaction. Most banks provide customers with a **bank statement**, a summary of the transactions that occurred during the month. The bank statement also shows the **balance**, the amount remaining in the account after each transaction.

Word Bank

transaction *any business done with the bank, such as a deposit or withdrawal*

withdrawal *the removal of money from a bank account*

bank statement *a monthly summary of a customer's transactions*

balance *the amount of money in a bank account*

MC BANK
Anycity, Anystate 01234

SAVINGS ACCOUNT STATEMENT

Account Number: 123456789
Date of Statement: April 1, 1998
Closing Balance: $463.00

Transactions This Month		Debit	Credit	Balance
Date	Description			
3/1	Opening Balance			
3/6	Deposit		$100.00	$328.00
3/19	Withdrawal	$15.00		$428.00
3/27	Deposit		$50.00	$413.00
				$463.00

43

Bank on It!

As you've probably noticed, banks are found in many different places, from main streets to supermarkets. There are banks in every country in the world. Did you know, though, that there are different kinds of banks? There are commercial banks, savings banks, and credit unions. Although banks generally serve either businesses or individuals, all banks offer similar services.

Commercial Banks Commercial banks were originally created to meet the needs of businesses. Today, most banks are commercial banks. They deal with individuals and with businesses. Commercial banks offer a variety of services. These services include checking accounts, savings accounts, and loans.

Savings Banks Savings banks were founded to give working people a place to save their money. Today, these banks are similar to commercial banks except that they mostly offer savings accounts and loans, so people can buy homes. Loans for buying homes are called **mortgages**.

Credit Unions Credit unions were started to help people borrow money. A group of people who had a common bond—for example, workers in a steel mill—pooled their savings. Like commercial banks, credit unions offer checking accounts, savings accounts, and loans. Unlike commercial banks, credit unions are nonprofit. This means that any profits the credit union makes are shared with the members.

> What's a savings account? What's a checking account? Just keep reading to find out!

SAVINGS ACCOUNT STATEMENT

A Matter of Fact
Did you ever have a piggy bank? Did you know its name has nothing to do with the animal? The piggy bank got its name from a kind of clay called *pygg*. Years ago, people stored their money in clay jars for safekeeping. These jars were called pygg banks. Eventually, the name changed to "piggy bank," and people actually began making them in the shape of a pig.

MC Bank
MC BANK

Banks, Piggy Banks

The Banks' Bank

As you read before, the Federal Reserve is the central bank of the United States. Most countries have a central bank to help regulate money. The Fed is not a typical bank, though. You can't deposit money there—but banks can. The Fed controls the money supply for the entire country. It does this by lending money to banks when they need it, but controlling the amount of money it lends.

Just as banks charge interest to customers who borrow money, the Fed charges interest to banks for borrowing money. But just as you wouldn't want to borrow money when interest rates are high, neither do banks. When the interest rate is high, banks borrow less money. That means there is less money in **circulation**—that is, there is less money available to use. It's up to the Fed to make sure that the total amount of money in circulation in the country is just right—not too much, not too little.

> The Federal Reserve System was created by an act of Congress in 1913.

> Wow! That's some act!

Banking—It's a Career

It takes a lot of people to run a bank. Each job requires different responsibilities and different levels of education. Some examples are listed below.

High School Degree

- A **teller** withdraws and deposits money for customers.
- A **security officer** maintains safety at the bank.
- A **proof machine operator** runs equipment at the bank and subtracts money from bank accounts.

College or Graduate Degree

- A **loan officer** arranges loans to businesses and individuals.
- An **accountant** keeps the financial records for a bank.
- A **lawyer** attends to a bank's legal matters.

A Penny for Your Thoughts

Sometimes, banks need extra money to meet their customers' demands. They get this cash from their regional Federal Reserve Bank. At what times of year do you think bank customers withdraw large sums of money?

Word Bank

mortgage *a loan given to pay for a house or building*

circulation *money that is available for use*

45

At Your Service

Banks earn money by investing their own money and by charging customers money, or **fees**, for different bank services. Like other businesses, banks are always looking for new customers. More customers mean more money for the bank. So banks offer services and conveniences they think will be attractive to consumers. These include special accounts and loans with low interest rates.

Safe and Sound

When you put money in a bank, you can be sure it is safe. Money is kept in steel vaults, which can only be opened by certain people, under very tight security. Did you know that bank vaults are fireproof?

But what happens if your bank is robbed or just goes out of business? A government agency called the FDIC, or Federal Deposit Insurance Corporation, will give you your money. By federal law, banks must insure customer accounts up to $100,000 with the FDIC.

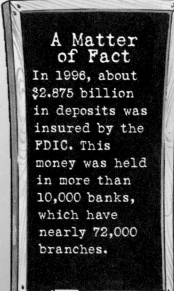

A Matter of Fact
In 1996, about $2.875 billion in deposits was insured by the FDIC. This money was held in more than 10,000 banks, which have nearly 72,000 branches.

Personal Treasures

If banks are such safe places to keep your money, why not keep other valuable items there, too? Well, you can! Many banks allow you to keep things like jewelry or important papers in a **safe-deposit box** at the bank. For a yearly fee, the bank will give you your own fireproof box and key. The bank keeps your safe-deposit box in a huge walk-in vault. Most safe-deposit boxes are about the same size as a shoe box. What would *you* put in a safe-deposit box?

safe-deposit boxes

Word Bank

fee *money charged for a service*

safe-deposit box *a place to keep special items in a bank*

Count on Them!

So Where's the Money?

Here's an interesting fact: Most of the money on deposit in the bank isn't really there—it's just a computer entry! This is because banks only need to keep a small amount of deposits in cash. What happens if a lot of people want to withdraw large sums of money from the bank at the same time? The bank orders cash from its Federal Reserve bank.

Look! No Paycheck!

When do you think a lot of people go to the bank? If you guessed on "payday," you're probably right! Many people receive a **check** from their company when they are paid. A check is a piece of paper that tells the bank to pay the person named on the check the amount of money specified. Did you know that many companies now offer **direct deposit** of paychecks? With this service, the company electronically deposits an employee's paycheck into his or her bank account. Sometime in the future, people won't have to use cash or checks at all!

A Penny for Your Thoughts

Some banks charge a fee for PC banking. Others encourage customers to try PC banking by making it available free of charge. How do you think PC banking benefits the bank or the customer?

Home-Based Banking

So you don't want to walk to the bank? If you have a personal computer (PC), and a modem (which lets your computer send messages over a phone line), you may not have to. **PC banking** lets you manage your money from home by linking your computer directly to your bank's computer. You can check your account balance, transfer money from one account to another, open new accounts—even pay bills electronically! You can do almost anything you can do at the bank, except make cash deposits or withdrawals.

Word Bank

check *a written order to a bank to pay a specified amount of money to a specified person or company, from money on deposit with the bank*

direct deposit *electronic deposit of checks in the bank*

PC banking *using a home or office computer to carry out bank transactions*

47

Don't tell anyone your PIN! Keep it a secret.

A Bank in Your Pocket—
The ATM Card

Do you have cash in your bank account that you need? Is the bank closed? Don't worry. It's not a problem if you have access to an **automated-teller machine (ATM)**. An ATM takes the place of human tellers. Unlike people, though, ATMs work 24 hours a day, 7 days a week, without a break. This means that you can use an ATM whenever it's convenient for you. You'll find ATMs in bank lobbies and in other accessible places around town.

Do you know what happens when you put your **ATM card** in the ATM? When your card is inserted, you are asked to enter a "secret code." This is your **personal identification number (PIN)**. If the ATM does not recognize your PIN, you will not be able to carry out any transactions at the ATM.

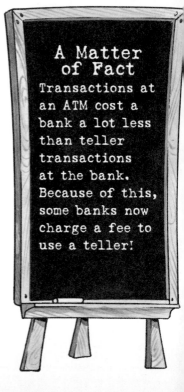

A Matter of Fact
Transactions at an ATM cost a bank a lot less than teller transactions at the bank. Because of this, some banks now charge a fee to use a teller!

If you lose your ATM card, let the bank know right away.

Always know how much is in your account. Keep track of all transactions you make, including any charges or fees.

Word Bank
automated-teller machine (ATM) *a machine that performs most of the banking operations that a human teller can*

ATM card *a bank card that allows customers to use an ATM machine*

personal identification number (PIN) *a code that activates an ATM card*

Now I'm Here, What Can I Do?

What kinds of banking can you do at an ATM? You can make deposits and withdrawals. You can check your account balance. You can transfer money between accounts. The machine will give you a receipt for the transaction just made and tell you your new balance. Be careful! Some banks charge a fee each time you use an ATM.

No Cash? No Problem!

Suppose you want to make a purchase. You don't have enough cash with you, but you do have the money in your checking account. You could use a bank **debit card**. A debit is money subtracted from an account. When you use your debit card, money is taken from your checking account to pay for something. You can also use a debit card at an ATM for your banking transactions, just as you would an ATM card. Sometimes an ATM card can be used as a debit card, too!

It's Not Magic—
How a Debit Card Works

When you use your debit card at a store, the shopkeeper slides your card through the card-reading machine. The machine contacts your bank electronically to make sure there's enough money in your checking account to pay for your purchase. If you do have enough money, that amount is automatically subtracted from your account and sent to the store's account to pay for your purchase.

Suppose you have $20.00 in your checking account and you want to buy something with your debit card that costs $18.50. That amount will be subtracted from your checking account, leaving you with a balance of $1.50. What if you only had $15.00 in your checking account? Then the store will not let you use your debit card to make that purchase. How could you still make the purchase?

Word Bank

debit card *a bank card that allows a person to withdraw money electronically from a checking account*

Not Everyone Banks

Cash and Carry

Banks offer a lot of services, but these services cost money. Some banks charge customers a monthly service fee for having a checking account. Other banks charge fees to customers who do not maintain a **minimum balance** in their accounts. That means that customers must keep a certain amount of money in the account. Sometimes the minimum balance may be thousands of dollars!

UNITED STATES POSTAL MONEY ORDER
15-800 / 000
***5*00
6666270379? 970916 079450
U.S. DOLLARS AND CENTS
POST OFFICE
SERIAL NUMBER
YEAR, MONTH, DAY
CHECKWRITER IMPRINT AREA
PAY TO: Fast Photo
ADDRESS: 9863 West Street
Anycity, Anystate 01234
COD NO. OR USED FOR: School Picture Reprint
FROM: Jane Dough
ADDRESS: 123 Greenbacks Way
Anycity, Anystate 01234
NEGOTIABLE ONLY IN THE U.S. AND POSSESSIONS
6666 270379?
00000800

Some people can't afford or don't need personal checking accounts. Suppose you didn't have a checking account, but you needed to pay some bills. What would you do? You could pay your bills with cash. But what if you needed to mail your payments? If your mail was lost or stolen, your cash would be gone! Instead, you could buy a **money order** at a bank or post office for a small fee. Like a check, a money order can only be cashed by the person whose name is on it. Unlike a check, money orders can be cashed anywhere they are sold.

50

Cashing In

Many people in the United States don't use banks at all. Some people can't afford, or choose not to pay, banking fees. Others may have work that keeps them moving from place to place. Without a bank account, it's not easy to **cash** a check—that is, to exchange the check for cash. What's the answer? A check-cashing business.

In exchange for cashing a check, the check-cashing business charges a fee, usually a portion of the dollar amount of the check. So check-cashing businesses provide instant cash to people without bank accounts. Without this service, many people could not cash their checks.

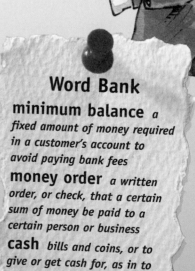

Word Bank
minimum balance *a fixed amount of money required in a customer's account to avoid paying bank fees*
money order *a written order, or check, that a certain sum of money be paid to a certain person or business*
cash *bills and coins, or to give or get cash for, as in to cash a check*

Fast Cash

Where can you go to borrow money if you need money right away? Borrowing money from a bank takes time. You need to apply for a loan and then wait for approval from the bank. What else can you do? One answer is to go to a **pawnshop**. Pawnshops are stores where you can leave something of value, such as a guitar or a camera, in exchange for a loan. The **pawnbroker**, who owns the pawnshop, will give you the money, along with a pawn ticket. With the ticket, property can be reclaimed for the amount of the loan, plus interest. However, there is a time limit to repay the loan. If the loan is not repaid, the pawnbroker keeps your property.

On Borrowed Time

A pawnshop loan can benefit both parties. The person needing money gets the money and the chance to "buy back" his or her property at a later date. The pawnbroker has something that is worth more than the cash loan just made. If the owner doesn't claim the property, the pawnbroker can sell the property for more than he or she paid for it. Today, there are fewer pawnshops than there used to be. That's because many people now have other means to pay for things when cash is scarce. You'll learn about those later on.

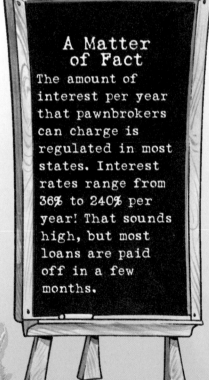

A Matter of Fact
The amount of interest per year that pawnbrokers can charge is regulated in most states. Interest rates range from 36% to 240% per year! That sounds high, but most loans are paid off in a few months.

Word Bank
pawnshop *a place to leave an item of value in exchange for a loan*
pawnbroker *a person who lends money at a specified interest rate to people who leave items as security*

Take Your Pick!

Count on It!

According to the Federal Reserve, there is about $525 billion in coins and bills in circulation today. How long would it take to count that amount if it takes 12 days without stopping to count to a million?

WOW, $525,000,000,000! That much money in hundred-dollar bills would be about 129,000 times taller than the Sears Tower, one of the tallest buildings in the world!

How does she know that?

Deposits and Withdrawals

Imagine your bank account was down to $75.00. You make 3 deposits of different amounts and 1 withdrawal. You now have $95.00. Yippee! How did you do it?

Break the Bank

Make your folks an offer they can't refuse. Tell them you'll walk the dog or take out the garbage each day for a month. Tell them they can pay you $20 for the month, or a penny the first day, two cents the second day, four cents the next day, eight cents the next day, and so on. Which offer should they accept?

52

Hint: It takes 233 stacked bills to equal one inch. The Sears Tower is 1,454 feet tall.

Chapter 5

Savings Accounts and Checking Accounts

It's your money. Make a home for it!

Making money is hard work. But figuring out what to do with it can seem even harder. What do you do with it? Most people put money in the bank.

How do banks help you manage money?
What kind of a savings account is best for you?
How do you write checks and balance a checkbook?
What's the difference between bank checks, traveler's checks, cashier's checks, and bounced checks?

In this chapter you'll learn how to make money work for *you*.

Savings Accounts—

Save Now, Play Later

Do you like to spend money? Of course—who doesn't? But by now you've realized that it's important to save money for those little emergencies and the big and little things that you want. Sometimes you need to put off spending now in order to save for the future.

Stashing Your Cash

Where's the safest place to stash your cash? You can keep your money in a piggy bank, or you can hide it under your mattress. But if it just sits there, you are actually losing money! As you learned earlier, if you keep money in a savings account, the bank pays interest on your money. Your interest will earn interest, making you even more money!

54

Keeping your cash at home may seem like a smart move, but what happens if there's a fire? Or the money is lost or stolen?

Or if somebody like me sinks his teeth into it!

A Matter of Fact

During the gold rush days in the late 1800s, a rich woman put a lot of bills inside her wood-burning stove for safekeeping. She figured that burglars would never think to look there. But the woman forgot to tell her husband. One day her husband lit the stove—and their whole fortune went up in smoke!

It All Adds Up

Time to Open an Account

So you've decided to open a savings account. What do you do next? At the bank you'll probably fill out a signature card. To make sure you are who you say you are, you'll need identification, such as a birth certificate. You will also need to tell the bank your Social Security number. If you're under 18, a parent or guardian will need to help you open an account.

You Have to Start Somewhere

Sometimes the bank requires a certain amount of money, called a **minimum deposit**, to open an account. The minimum deposit may be as little as $5 or as much as $100 or more. It all depends on the bank you choose. Why do you think some banks want a minimum deposit? It's because it costs the bank money to hire the people to help you open a bank account, and then to manage it.

A Penny for Your Thoughts

Putting money in a bank is one way to save money. But you can save money by being careful, too. For example, you can turn off unneeded lights to lower your electric bill. You can make a meal at home instead of going out to eat. What are some other ways you can cut back spending to save money?

Word Bank

minimum deposit *the least amount of money required to open an account*

55

A Penny Saved
Is a Penny Earned

Did you know that there are three different kinds of savings accounts? Each type of account has different features and may pay a different amount of interest. Take a look!

Statement Savings Account A statement savings account is the most common bank savings account today. With this type of account, the bank sends you a statement once a month. The statement shows how much money you deposited or withdrew from your savings account, how much interest you earned, and how much money is in the account.

Passbook Accounts Do you always want to know how much money is in your account and what transactions have happened? Then a passbook account is for you. With this kind of account, every transaction you make, including interest your money has earned, is recorded in your passbook. Each time you make a deposit or a withdrawal, you give your passbook to the bank teller. The teller records each transaction in your passbook. Passbook accounts usually pay the same amount of interest as statement savings accounts.

ALWAYS VERIFY ENTRY BEFORE LEAVING WINDOW
THIS BOOK MUST BE PRESENTED FOR EVERY DEPOSIT OR WITHDRAWAL
IF LOST, NOTIFY BANK IMMEDIATELY

DATE	MEMO	DEPOSIT	WITHDRAWAL	INTEREST	BALANCE
					$350.00
01	03JUL	$350.00		.91	$350.91
02	01AUG				$250.91
03	18AUG		$100.00		$251.57
04	01SEP			.66	$336.57
05	26SEP	$ 85.00			$337.45
06	01OCT			.88	$437.45
07	25OCT	$100.00			

Certificate of Deposit (CD) What if you have some money that you don't plan to use for a while? You can buy a certificate of deposit. You deposit money, called **principal**, in the bank for a specific amount of time, such as six months or a year. You are not allowed to withdraw the money until the end of the time period—or else you pay a penalty! But because the bank knows how long it will have your money, it can lend it and not worry about when you will need it. This means you get more interest than you would in a regular savings account.

> Wow! I've got a CD!

> So do I!

CERTIFICATE OF DEPOSIT

CD PLAYER

Money Market Account What kind of savings account pays more interest than a regular savings account *and* lets you withdraw money by writing checks? A money market account! It's a great deal, but there are some limitations. You can usually write only a limited number of checks each month from this account. Also, money market accounts usually require a large minimum balance. Since you can withdraw your money at any time, banks pay a little less interest for this kind of account than for a CD.

A Penny for Your Thoughts

What kind of account would you choose if you were saving for your college education?

Individual Retirement Account (IRA)
Do you know what an IRA is? It's a savings account for your **retirement**. You are allowed to put a part of your income into an IRA each year. You do not have to pay taxes on this money until you take out the money. When you are retired and withdraw the money, the taxes you pay will be less.

Word Bank

principal *a sum of money in an account, not including interest*

retirement *when a person gives up his or her job, often because of age*

Parents Can Bank on It

Sometimes, parents start saving for their children. Parents can open a special savings account called a trust account. Over the years, they can deposit money into it on a regular basis. When the children are old enough (usually 21 years old), they take over the account. By then the account has earned a lot of interest, because no money has been withdrawn! The children can use the trust account for big expenses like tuition or a mortgage. What are some reasons why parents might or might not open a trust account for their children?

A Matter of Fact

Americans are really starting to save for retirement! In 1997, over $330 billion was stashed away in retirement accounts in U.S. banks. That's up from only $6.6 billion in 1977.

You'll check up on checks next.

Checks and

Time for a Check Up

Many people choose to keep their money in two bank accounts: a savings account and a checking account. Do you know the difference? A checking account lets you keep your money in the bank, just like a savings account. But you usually have to be at least 18 years old to open a checking account. And the bank probably won't pay you interest on your money. Instead, it will let you write checks from that account. And checks can really come in handy!

Suppose you are buying a new bicycle for $150. That's a lot of money to carry around. So instead of carrying around the cash, you can write a check. A check tells your bank how much money to take from your bank account to give to someone else.

So all you need to carry is your checkbook—and maybe a pen! Don't write checks in pencil. The information could be erased or changed. Paying bills by check is a good idea. Do you know why? One reason is that a check is proof of payment.

This is the **date** you are writing the check.

This is the **amount** in numerals.

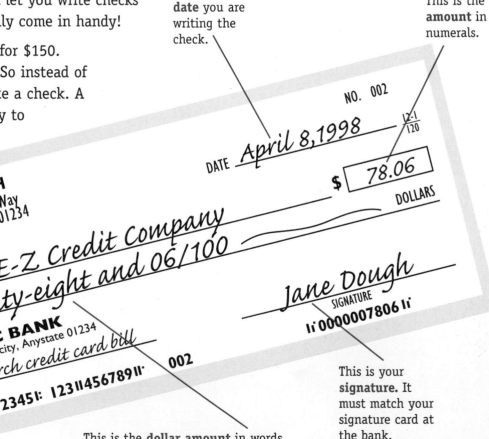

NO. 002

DATE April 8, 1998   12-1/120

$ 78.06

DOLLARS

JANE DOUGH
123 Greenbacks Way
Anycity, Anystate 01234

PAY TO THE ORDER OF   E-Z Credit Company

seventy-eight and 06/100

MC BANK
Anycity, Anystate 01234

FOR March credit card bill

I:000012345I: 123II456789II· 002

Jane Dough
SIGNATURE

Ii·0000007806 Ii·

This is the **name** of the person or company you want to pay.

This is your **signature.** It must match your signature card at the bank.

This is the **dollar amount** in words and the cents in numerals. Always draw a line to fill the whole space. This prevents anyone from adding anything to your amount.

Balances

Keeping Tabs on Your Checks

So, you've opened up a checking account, and you're writing checks. Are you sure you have enough money in your account to cover all the checks you're writing? To make sure that you do, record every check you write. Some checkbooks make carbon copies of each check you write. Most checkbooks have a separate section called a **register** in which you record the checks you write. Your check register is like a homemade bank statement!

A Balancing Act

Keeping accurate records of the checks you write is important. To make sure your records are accurate, you need to balance your checkbook monthly. This means that what your bank statement says should match your own records. Why do you think it's called balancing?

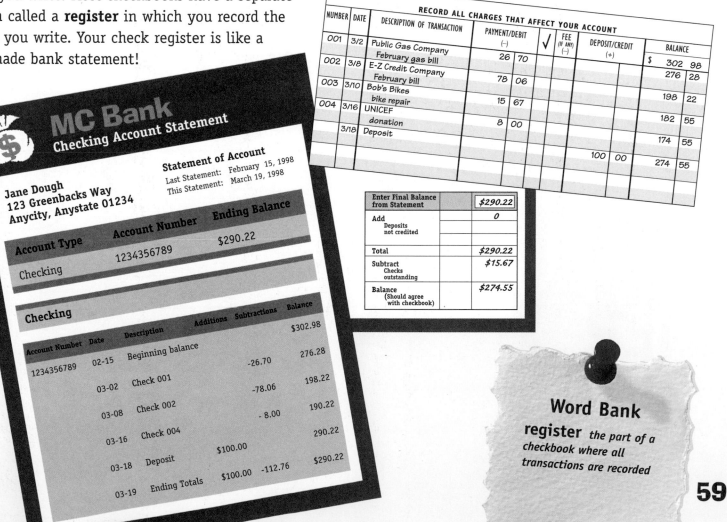

NUMBER	DATE	DESCRIPTION OF TRANSACTION	PAYMENT/DEBIT (−)	✓	FEE (IF ANY) (−)	DEPOSIT/CREDIT (+)	BALANCE
001	3/2	Public Gas Company February gas bill	26 70				$ 302 98
002	3/8	E-Z Credit Company February bill	78 06				276 28
003	3/10	Bob's Bikes bike repair	15 67				198 22
004	3/16	UNICEF donation	8 00				182 55
	3/18	Deposit				100 00	174 55
							274 55

Enter Final Balance from Statement	$290.22
Add Deposits not credited	0
Total	$290.22
Subtract Checks outstanding	$15.67
Balance (Should agree with checkbook)	$274.55

MC Bank
Checking Account Statement

Statement of Account
Last Statement: February 15, 1998
This Statement: March 19, 1998

Jane Dough
123 Greenbacks Way
Anycity, Anystate 01234

Account Type	Account Number	Ending Balance
Checking	1234356789	$290.22

Checking

Account Number	Date	Description	Additions	Subtractions	Balance
1234356789	02-15	Beginning balance			$302.98
	03-02	Check 001		-26.70	276.28
	03-08	Check 002		-78.06	198.22
	03-16	Check 004		- 8.00	190.22
	03-18	Deposit	$100.00		290.22
	03-19	Ending Totals	$100.00	-112.76	$290.22

Word Bank
register the part of a checkbook where all transactions are recorded

59

The Life of a Check

Moving Right Along

Today, most money is never seen or touched. It is transferred from bank to bank electronically. This is possible because of computers. Computers speed up the way banks do business. It's a lot faster to have a computer transfer money than to carry millions of pieces of paper and coins from one bank to another—especially when some of the banks are halfway around the world! Part of this movement of money is done by checks that people write. With a check, money moves from one person to another, but no bills or coins change hands!

A Matter of Fact
If you add all of the costs of moving checks through the banking system, including the cost of paper, printing, and mailing, the total is about 80¢ per check.

2 The store owner deposits the check in the store's account at its San Francisco branch.

1 A girl in New York buys in-line skates from the catalog of a sports store in San Francisco. Her mother mails a check to pay for them.

6 The New York bank then tells its clearinghouse to subtract the amount from its account.

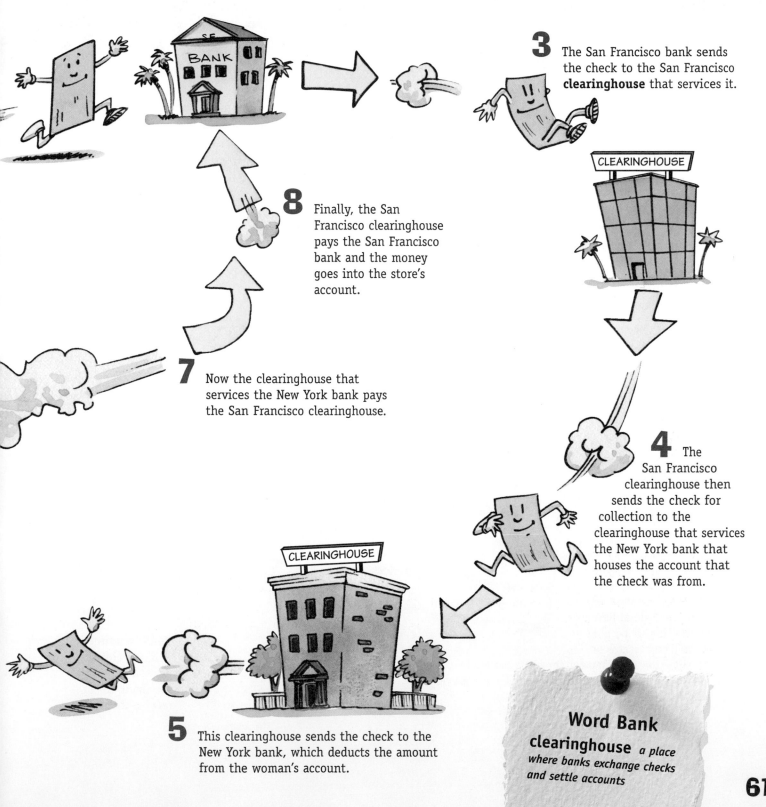

3 The San Francisco bank sends the check to the San Francisco **clearinghouse** that services it.

CLEARINGHOUSE

8 Finally, the San Francisco clearinghouse pays the San Francisco bank and the money goes into the store's account.

7 Now the clearinghouse that services the New York bank pays the San Francisco clearinghouse.

4 The San Francisco clearinghouse then sends the check for collection to the clearinghouse that services the New York bank that houses the account that the check was from.

CLEARINGHOUSE

5 This clearinghouse sends the check to the New York bank, which deducts the amount from the woman's account.

Word Bank

clearinghouse *a place where banks exchange checks and settle accounts*

Deciphering the
Check Code

Checks are processed by high-speed computers that read the instructions printed in code on the bottom of the check in special ink. This ink can be magnetized so the computer can read the code. About 2,400 checks can be sorted in one minute!

Reading a check? That doesn't sound too exciting!

I think I'll stick to reading mystery novels.

Routing number
This number is used to manually process a check.

Check number

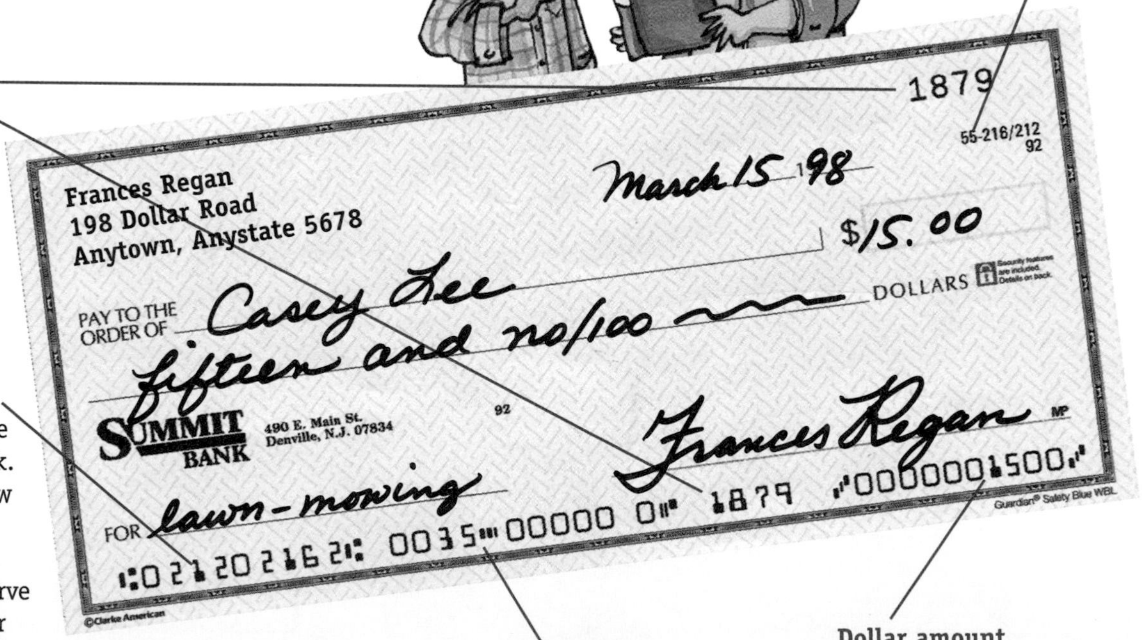

Check-routing numbers
These numbers identify the bank that issued the check. The first two numbers show the bank's Federal Reserve district. The third number identifies the Federal Reserve branch. The fourth number shows the bank's state- or special-collection arrangement (how the money is to be collected). The last number verifies that all the previous numbers are correct.

Bank account number

Dollar amount
This amount is printed by the first bank to receive the check.

Frances Regan
198 Dollar Road
Anytown, Anystate 5678

1879

55-216/212
92

March 15 98

$15.00

PAY TO THE ORDER OF *Casey Lee*

fifteen and no/100 ———— DOLLARS

SUMMIT BANK
490 E. Main St.
Denville, N.J. 07834

92

Frances Regan MP

FOR *lawn-mowing*

⑆021202162⑆ 0035⑈00000 0⑈ 1879 ⑉000000150 0⑈

©Clarke American

62

Speaking

Depositor's endorsement
In order to deposit or cash a check, you must **endorse** it, or sign your name on the back. Many banks also require customers to write their bank-account number on the check as well.

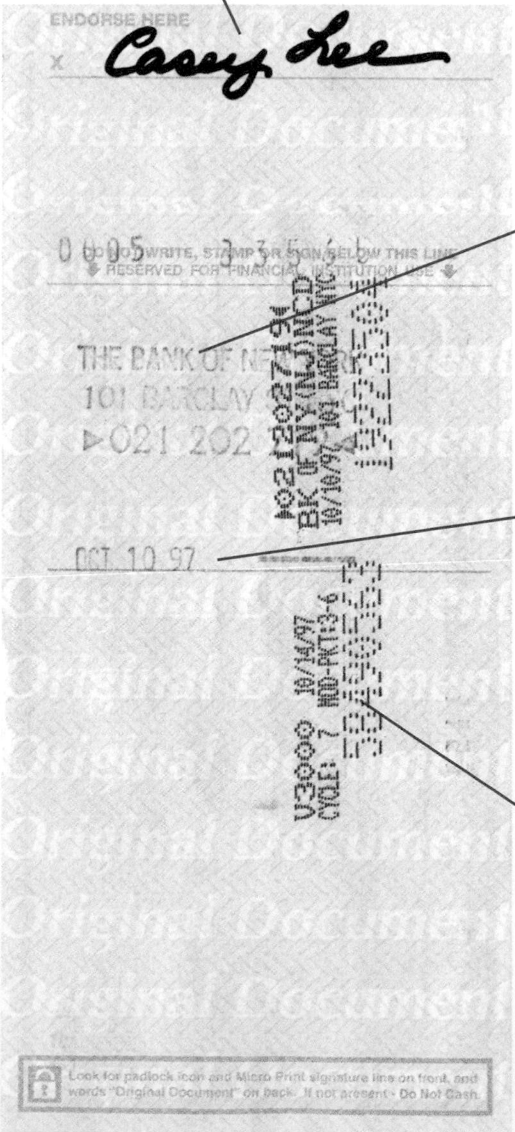

ENDORSE HERE
X Casey Lee
DO NOT WRITE, STAMP OR SIGN BELOW THIS LINE
RESERVED FOR FINANCIAL INSTITUTION USE
OCT 10 97
Look for padlock icon and Micro Print signature line on front, and words "Original Document" on back. If not present - Do Not Cash.

Bank stamp
This bank is where the check was processed.

Process date stamp

Payment stamp
This indicates that your bank has certified that you have enough money in the bank to pay this check and that it has been paid.

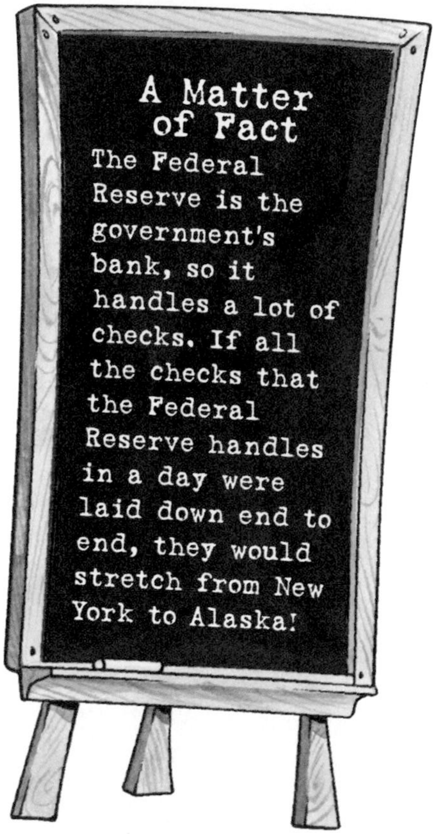

A Matter of Fact
The Federal Reserve is the government's bank, so it handles a lot of checks. If all the checks that the Federal Reserve handles in a day were laid down end to end, they would stretch from New York to Alaska!

Word Bank

endorse *to sign your name on the back of a check before depositing it*

Check It Out

Bounced checks and balanced checkbooks? What's next?

Checking Checks

Warning! If you write a check to your friend Mary, you must have enough money in your checking account to pay the amount on the check. If you don't have enough money, you have "insufficient funds," and the check will be returned to you. If this happens, you will have to pay a fee to the bank for this check. Some people call this kind of check a rubber check, or a **bounced check,** because it goes back to the person who wrote it. If you bounce a check and don't pay the person you gave the check to with cash or a new check, you can end up in jail.

A Matter of Fact
Almost 80% of all store sales in the United States are made to people who pay with either checks or credit cards. So, what percent of people pay with cash?

Traveling With Checks

You've probably seen ads on TV about people on vacation who lose their cash. How do you think travelers avoid this? If you said traveler's checks, you're right! For a small fee you can buy **traveler's checks** at most banks and credit unions. You can even buy the checks in a foreign currency. Traveler's checks are a safe way to carry money to places that won't accept credit cards or personal checks. Traveler's checks work just like cash. If you pay for something that costs eight dollars with a ten-dollar traveler's check, you'd get two dollars change.

Word Bank
bounced check *a check returned by the bank for lack of funds*
traveler's check *a special kind of check used by travelers instead of cash*

It's Official!

Suppose you are an adult who wants to buy a car that costs $8,000. If you want to write a check, the car dealer may require you to have your check guaranteed by a bank. You could have the bank certify, or guarantee, one of your own checks. The bank does this only after checking the current balance of your account to make sure you have enough money to cover the check. You could also purchase a single check from the bank, called a **cashier's check**. A cashier's check is just like a certified check, except that the money comes from the bank's account after the money is transferred from your account. Either way, the car dealer has the bank's word that the check can be cashed.

Why Not Cash?

Checks are everywhere! They have become the most common medium of exchange in the U.S. People write checks more often than they use cash. Checks aren't necessarily better than cash, but in many ways they are easier. Checks are safer to send or carry than cash because cash is more easily stolen, and a check has value only if it is signed by the owner of the checking account.

A Penny for Your Thoughts

Now that you know all about checking accounts, do you think that you would rather write a check or use a debit card? Why?

No Need for Checks?

The use of debit cards has reduced the use of checks and has also made banking cheaper. In the future you may not even need checks. You'll just call up a store and place an order for something. The store will contact your bank electronically. The bank will use its computers to automatically take money from your account and put it into the seller's account. This is called **electronic funds transfer**. In fact, we already transfer money electronically when we use an ATM or pay bills by computer. What are some advantages and disadvantages to doing business this way?

Word Bank

cashier's check *a check that you buy from a bank that is guaranteed by the bank*

electronic funds transfer *the movement of money from one account to another via computer*

65

Take Your Pick!

It's Your Money

Suppose you receive $10 allowance each week. Each week you put $4 in your savings account, $3 in your checking account, and keep $3 for spending money. How long would it take you to add $20 to your savings account?

Logical Savings

How much does each person have in his or her savings account?

It All Adds Up (or Does It?)

Suppose you deposit $100 in a bank. Each month you receive 5% interest on your $100. Each month you take out $5 for spending money. How long will it take until your balance reaches $150?

Once Upon a Time . . .

Imagine that you're a check. Tell a funny story describing your travels and adventures from the bank to someone's checkbook to a business to a clearinghouse and back to the bank. What happens to you? Whom do you meet? What kind of trouble do you get into along the way?

I have $3 more than you in my account.

I have $11 less than you in my account.

I have twice as much as you in my account.

I can't even open an account!

Chapter 6

All About Credit

What it is, what it's not, and how to use it!

I wonder if I have enough credit to buy this computer.

Some people couldn't live without them. Other people refuse to use them. What are they? Credit cards!

What is credit? What's the difference between credit cards and checks?

How old do you have to be to get a credit card?

What are some advantages to using credit?

What are some disadvantages?

Take the time to find the answers to these questions and more in this chapter. When you're finished reading, give yourself some credit for learning all the facts.

It's In-credit-ible!

Talking Credit

Did you know that you can buy something without money? No, it's not free. It's **credit!** Credit means that someone is willing to lend you money and give you time to pay it back, usually for a fee or with interest. Credit lets you buy now and pay later. Consumers use credit to buy the things they need or want, such as houses, clothing, or cars. Businesses use credit to expand and grow. Even federal, state, and local governments use credit to build and repair things like roads, bridges, and schools.

LOW INTEREST

BUY NOW PAY LATER

Low Monthly Payments

In Search of... Credit

Where can you get credit? Banks, businesses, and individuals can give credit. A friend of yours who buys you a snack and lets you pay him or her back later is giving you credit. He or she trusts you to pay the money back.

Some stores will allow you to buy very expensive items on credit. However, you might have to pay a certain portion of the **debt**, or the money you owe, as a **down payment**. You pay the balance, or the rest of the bill, in small amounts each month, called **installments**, plus interest. So the item actually costs more than its original price. What's the point, you ask? You can get what you need or want now, even if you don't have the money to pay with cash.

Banking on Credit

Banks give credit to their customers in lots of ways, such as mortgages, installment loans, credit cards, and **lines of credit**. A line of credit means that a prearranged amount of money is available for you in the bank whenever you need to use it. Any money you borrow, you must repay, with interest. But if you don't borrow any money, you pay nothing. For instance, if you have a $5,000 line of credit and you only use $1,000, you will only have to pay back $1,000, plus any interest. On the other hand, with mortgages and loans, you get all of the money at one time upfront.

Word Bank

credit *money loaned, usually for a fee, that must be repaid*

debt *money owed to a person or business*

down payment *an amount of money paid as an initial lump sum payment for a debt*

installment *partial payment of a debt, paid regularly*

line of credit *an agreed-upon amount of money that can be borrowed from a bank*

Checking
You Out

Will a bank give credit to anyone who asks for it? No. State laws vary, but you usually have to be 18 or 21 to apply for credit. Also, a bank will only give credit to someone it feels sure will pay back the loan. What are some ways banks know you'll pay them back? One way banks do this is to run a credit check on you to make sure you pay your bills on time. If you've never borrowed from a bank before, you may also need **collateral** for your loan. Collateral is something valuable, like jewelry, stocks, or bonds, that you give to the bank to hold until the loan is paid off. If you **default**, or don't repay the loan, the bank can sell the collateral. You may also be required to have someone, such as a parent with a good credit history, **cosign** the loan. This means that your parent is responsible for repaying the loan if you can't.

A Matter of Fact
The word *credit* comes from the Latin word *creditus*, meaning "to trust." When someone lends you money, he or she is trusting you to repay it.

Shopping Around

What's the most important thing you do before you make a major purchase? Why, shop around! That way you're sure you're paying the best price. When you need credit, the same rule applies. Shop around. Check what different banks charge. Find the different conditions, or **credit terms**, for the credit that you want.

Some banks charge customers to apply for credit. Other banks offer lower interest rates but charge a fee if your payment is late. Interest rates and loan terms may also vary among banks. Remember, there is always a trade-off between the amount of time you take to repay money, and the amount of money you pay each month. If you can only afford a small monthly payment, it will take you longer to repay your debt. The longer you take to repay, the more interest you'll pay to the bank.

Word Bank
collateral *property, such as a house or car, that a borrower promises to give to a lender in case of a loan default*

default *to fail to repay a loan*

cosign *to sign a document for another person, indicating responsibility if the borrower defaults*

credit terms *conditions of credit, such as interest rates and fees*

69

What a Card!

What's plastic, flat, about the size of a playing card, and can be used like money? If you answered "a credit card," you're right! Millions of Americans have **credit cards**. Credit cards are used to pay for vacations, clothing, books, computers, groceries, and even taxes! You can buy goods and services wherever your card is accepted and pay for them later. What a deal! Or is it?

There are strings attached to credit cards. Unless you pay the full amount you owe each month, the goods or services you buy with the credit card end up being more expensive than if you had paid for them with cash or a check. This happens because interest is added to the cost of your purchase. So a credit card should be used very carefully!

Where Do I Get One?

Banks are the main sources of credit cards. Bank-issued credit cards can be used at any business that accepts them. Many stores and service companies also issue credit cards. These cards can only be used at the store or company that issued them. But they work just the same as bank credit cards. People often have several credit cards: one or two from banks, and others from stores and companies they use often.

> Wow! I only have to pay $2 a month for all these biscuits!

> At that rate it will take 20 years to pay off the bill.

> You'd better eat slowly!

Walter Cavanagh

A Matter of Fact

The Guinness Book of World Records reports that Walter Cavanagh of Santa Clara, California, owns the largest number of credit cards. "Mr. Plastic Fantastic," as he likes to be called, has 1,356 different cards! He keeps them in the world's longest wallet—250 feet long and weighing $37\frac{1}{2}$ pounds!

Word Bank

credit card *a card that allows a person to make purchases on credit*

70

Credit

Why Do They Do It?

Why do banks and companies provide people with credit cards? Because they make money from them! Every month the bank sends cardholders a bill showing everything they bought with the card that month. Some banks allow cardholders to pay just part of the bill each month. If a cardholder chooses to pay part of the bill, he or she must pay interest to the bank on the amount of money that is still owed, plus interest on any new charges. Some cards don't charge interest at all. But you have to pay a membership fee each year, called an annual fee, and you have to pay the balance due each month on your bill.

It's in the Cards

How do the stores that accept bank credit cards get paid? After you make a purchase with your credit card, the store where you made the purchase contacts the bank that issued your credit card. The bank then pays the store for everything that is charged on the card. The bank also charges the store a fee for this service. The bank then bills you for the amount of the purchase. The bank pays the store, and you pay the bank.

Bonus!

Some credit card companies give you bonuses for using their card. Some let you earn "miles" for every dollar you charge on your card, which you can turn in to receive free plane tickets. Other companies donate money to charity whenever you charge something on your card. Some companies even give you consumer protection with any item you buy with your card. That means if you lose or break the item within a certain amount of time after you bought it, the credit card company will replace it for free! Or will it be free? Where does the credit card company get the money to replace the item? From the interest and fees it charges its customers—including you!

A Penny for Your Thoughts
Why are stores willing to pay the bank a fee to allow customers to use a credit card? What benefits does the store get? Do you think these benefits are worth it?

71

Payback Time

Remember bank statements? If you have a credit card, you also receive a monthly statement from the credit card company. Take a look at the credit card statement below.

Payment due
This is the date when you must make your next payment.

Previous balance
This is how much you owed last month.

Account This number is used by the bank to identify your account.

Payments, credits
This is how much you paid last month and how much money was credited to your account. If you didn't pay the whole balance, you will pay interest on the money you owe.

E-Z Credit Company

Account: 55512123434
Credit Limit: $500

Statement Date: 4/15
Payment Due: 5/07

Credit limit
This is the limit on the total amount of money you can charge.

	TOTAL
	$25.00
	25.00
Previous Balance	66.75
(-) Payments/Credits	0.00
(+) Purchases	66.75
(-) Finance Charges	
(=) New Balance	$10.00
Minimum Payment	

Purchases This is how much you charged on your card this month.

New balance This is how much you owe now.

Date	Transactions	Credits	Charges
		$25.00	
3/21	Payment		$45.25
3/26	X-Pressly for You Shop		$6.00
3/26	Pizza Plus		$15.50
4/06	Music Maniac		
Total of Credits and Charges		$25.00	$66.75

Charges
This is a detailed description of all of your purchases from the past month.

Minimum payment
This is the least amount of money you must pay this month.

Word Bank
credit limit *the amount of credit available to a person*

A Penny for Your Thoughts
What are some reasons you might not pay your entire balance when it's due? What are the dangers and costs of putting off full payment?

Cards or Checks?

When you use a credit card, you're really taking out a loan from a bank or a credit card company. The bank or company pays the store and then bills you for the money you charged to the credit card. If you pay by check, the money comes directly from your checking account. If you don't have the money, you can't make the purchase. But you pay a price for using the credit card—it's called interest!

Pay now?

Pay later?

Either way you have to pay.

A Matter of Fact
Americans have more than 500 million credit cards. More than half of those cards are VISA cards.

What's in Store for You?

What's the best way for you to get credit for the first time? Be responsible! You need to show the bank or credit card company that you're able to handle money. One way to show you are creditworthy is to get and keep a job. That way, the credit card company knows that you have a regular income available to pay your credit card bills. Another way to do this is to open a savings account and deposit money regularly. Then when you want to apply for credit, the savings account will show that you are a consistent customer. Paying bills on time is also important.

The easiest kind of credit to get for the first time is a department store credit card. Many stores have special charge accounts for teenagers. To open this kind of account, a parent or other adult must usually cosign. If you are old enough, the customer service department will give you an application to fill out.

So far, so good, but now to the most important part of a department store credit card application: the *Retail Installment Credit Agreement*. This agreement lets you know the terms of the credit agreement. It tells you whether you must pay your bill all at once or if you can pay in installments. The interest rate you'll be charged if you don't pay the whole bill is also explained. Now that you understand all this, you just need to wait for approval.

73

It Isn't Only Plastic

Credit—
Good Idea or Bad?

Credit cards make buying very easy. But a credit card is not a license to spend money. You should be careful not to charge more than you are able to pay. Credit cards themselves are also an expense. As you learned before, many cards charge a yearly fee. The interest rates for credit cards are usually much higher than the interest rates on bank loans. An unpaid credit card balance can build up interest pretty quickly. Here are some tips for being a wise credit user.

- Understand the terms of your credit agreement. Read it carefully. Find out exactly how much money you have to pay each month. Usually, the greater the amount that you charge, the more you have to pay.

- Save all the sales receipts from purchases you make on credit. Then you will have a record of how much money you have spent each month. You will also have a record in case the store makes a mistake with your bill.

- Don't use your credit card for every purchase. Pay cash when you can. Paying cash is always cheaper.

- Plan your purchases. If you know you need to buy several expensive items, try to spread out your buying over time. That way you won't have to pay a large credit card bill.

- Choose a few credit cards that you know you will use. It will be easier to keep track of your money, and you won't be paying lots of interest and annual fees.

A Matter of Fact

Can you imagine a credit card that thinks? One such "smart card" is being used in France today. These credit cards come with built-in computers that record each transaction made with the card. That makes record-keeping a whole lot easier!

I'm smarter than these guys.

Maybe, but being really smart means being respons with credit.

Don't Shop for Trouble

You've just received your credit card statement, and there's a charge on it for 15 pairs of basketball sneakers! And you don't even *like* basketball! Someone must have used your credit card, and now you have an enormous bill. What do you do? Under federal law, you are only required to pay $50 if your card is stolen and used by someone else. But if you lose your card or think it's been stolen, you must call the credit card company right away. They will cancel your card and give you a new one. Hopefully, they will catch the person who is going on an illegal shopping spree.

Do you know someone who has bought something over the phone or through a computer? You can pay for such a purchase with a credit card, but you must be careful. Other people can use your number to charge things, even without having your card. So, if you find an unexpected purchase on your monthly statement, be sure to call your credit card company right away.

It's Your Turn to Take the Credit

Every day you make decisions about money. Whether you're shopping for a computer or a pair of shoes, there are always things to consider. How much am I prepared to spend? Which is the best buy? Do I really need this? Do I need it *now*? Should I buy on credit, or wait until I have the cash and save money? There's a lot to think about.

Credit cards make buying things easy—sometimes too easy. You have to stay on your toes and be a smart "charger" as well as a smart shopper. You have to manage your own money—and your credit—and that takes a lot of planning. As you can see, there's a lot more to money than just dollars and cents!

A Penny for Your Thoughts

It used to be a custom in America for engaged couples to exchange coins as pledges of love. Do you think the idea of exchanging credit cards will ever catch on? Why or why not?

CREDIT CARD STATEMENT

SNEAKER HEAVEN $ 1,500

15 PAIR @ $100⁰⁰ EA

$ 1,500

Take Your Pick!

Extra Charge!

Many different businesses now offer credit cards. Phone companies, charitable organizations, and even baseball teams offer them. When you make purchases using these cards, you may receive benefits, like free phone calls, or money may be donated to a charitable organization. Which bonus would you like to get from a credit card?

Credit: Pro or Con?

In the chart are reasons why people like *and* dislike credit. But they're all mixed up. Decide which ones are advantages to having credit and which ones are disadvantages.

yearly fees

protection from theft

spending what you can't afford

accepted all over the world

good for emergencies

interest payments

Have a Bite!

Chez Chucky Menu

apple juice	small	$1.00
	large	$1.50
lemonade	small	$ .75
	large	$1.00
hamburger		$2.00
tuna		$2.50
fruit salad		$1.50
yogurt		$1.75

Charge your lunch on a credit card! What would you order for lunch from Chez Chucky? How much would it cost? Don't forget to add the tax and tip!

Chapter 7

The Big Picture of Money— The Economy!

What **is** it?
What does it **mean** to **you**?

ECONOMY. It's a big word. Everyone, from your family to the President, talks about it.

How does the economy work?
What is supply and demand?
What are inflation and recession?

This chapter will help you understand some of the big issues surrounding money. You'll see what it takes to start a business. You'll explore the relationships between buyers and sellers, prices and quantity—and more. When you've finished the chapter, you'll have a better idea about the big picture—the big picture of money, that is.

It's the Economy

Consumers and Producers

From the moment you spend your first dime, you are a consumer—someone who exchanges money for goods or services. It doesn't take much training or preparation to be a consumer. In fact, most people get into the habit of spending more easily than they do saving. Are you a saver, a spender, or both?

As a spender or consumer, you are faced with many choices—often very tempting ones. But it's your job to use your money wisely. You could say it's a full-time job. But there's another side to being a consumer. Most consumers are producers as well. Through work as individuals or as part of a company, people help produce all the goods and services that consumers use. The **economy** is how consumers and producers work together to produce and use all the things people want and need. An economy includes people, natural resources, and all the things people produce and consume.

Word Bank

economy *the way in which human resources and natural resources are used to produce goods and services*

Big, Bigger, Biggest

How well consumers and producers work together is one measure of how well the economy is doing. But a person can be involved in more than one economy. How can that be? A town or a state has a local economy, which is made up of the consumers and producers in that town or state. A country has a national economy, which is made up of all the consumers and producers from all parts of that country. An international economy is made up of the different goods and services produced and consumed by many different countries. Did you realize that you are a part of all these economies?

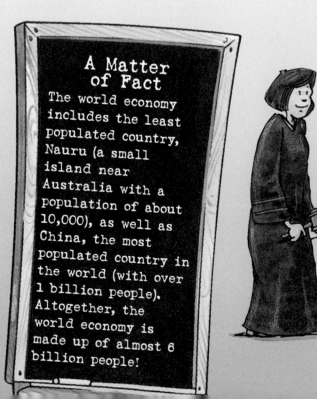

A Matter of Fact

The world economy includes the least populated country, Nauru (a small island near Australia with a population of about 10,000), as well as China, the most populated country in the world (with over 1 billion people). Altogether, the world economy is made up of almost 6 billion people!

A Sector Here, A Sector There

An economy is made up of different types of workers. Think of the adults in your family. What kind of work do they do? Some people work in the **private sector**, which means they work for themselves or for a company or business.

Did you know that the government is also an employer? The government hires people to run its offices and services. The government uses some of the money it collects from taxes to pay the salaries of these workers. People who work for the government work in the **public sector** of the economy.

A Penny for Your Thoughts

Suppose that you live in a town on the coast. You have a friend who lives in a town in the mountains. What types of jobs might be available in your town but not in your friend's town? What jobs might be found in both?

It's Only Natural

Think about the area you live in. What types of jobs are available near you? Why do you think people in your area do the jobs they do?

People's jobs have a lot to do with where they live. The geography and **natural resources** of a particular region often determine the kind of work that is available in that area. Natural resources such as oil or iron ore often determine related jobs and industries, such as mining and steel production.

PUBLIC

PRIVATE

Word Bank

private sector *the part of the economy produced by individuals and businesses*

public sector *the part of the economy produced by the government*

natural resource *a supply of something that is found naturally on Earth*

What's in a Business?

You are part of the national economy. You use goods and services, so you are a consumer. But how can you be a producer? You can by running or being part of a **business**. A business brings in money by selling goods or services. There are two basic types of businesses. A manufacturing business, like an in-line skate factory, makes and sells a product. In a service business, such as dry cleaning or home construction, someone does work in exchange for money or goods. What types of businesses have you been involved in?

It's Not Just Busy-ness

Have you ever started your own business? If so, you are an **entrepreneur**. An entrepreneur is someone who creates a business and often hires workers to help him or her. An entrepreneur makes the best use of natural resources as well as the talents and energies of workers to try to create a successful business.

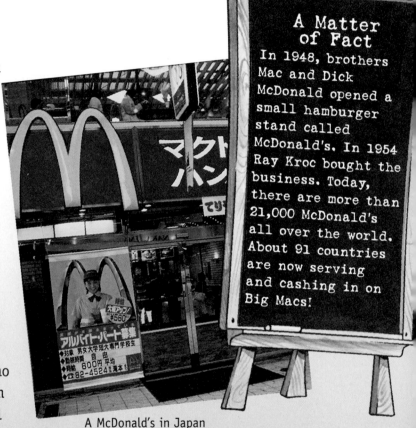

A Matter of Fact
In 1948, brothers Mac and Dick McDonald opened a small hamburger stand called McDonald's. In 1954 Ray Kroc bought the business. Today, there are more than 21,000 McDonald's all over the world. About 91 countries are now serving and cashing in on Big Macs!

A McDonald's in Japan

Word Bank

business *an enterprise that brings in money from selling goods or services*

entrepreneur *a person who creates and manages a business*

risk *the chance of loss*

Starting a business is hard work. It takes creativity, organizational skills, and courage. It means taking a **risk**. But it can be very rewarding if the business is a success. Many people are happy to run small businesses, and sometimes a small business can grow into a multimillion-dollar company!

Business

Mind Your New Business

Do you have an idea for a business? How are you going to get it up and running? First you'll want to find out if your business has a chance of succeeding. One way to check is by doing a **market survey**. A market survey asks people questions about their likes and dislikes. It asks what goods or services people would use, and how much they'd be willing to pay for them. The answers people give to the survey help business people decide whether or not to move forward with their plans.

This Business Is for the Dogs!

Suppose you wanted to start a dog-walking service. You have the time and you like dogs. But you're not sure if people need this service in your area, and if they do, what specific needs they have. Here's a market survey you could use to find out.

Word Bank

market survey *a questionnaire designed to find out what people think about a particular product or service*

MARKET SURVEY

yes no

- Do you have a dog? - - - - - - - - - - - ☐ ☐
- Do you walk your dog more than twice a day? - - - - - - - - - - - ☐ ☐
- Are you often too bone-tired to play with your dog? - - - - - - - - ☐ ☐
- Does your dog need more exercise? - -☐ ☐
- Would you pay someone to exercise your dog? - - - - - - - - - - - - - ☐ ☐
- Would you pay for this service more than once a week? - - - - - - - ☐ ☐
- Would you be interested in weekend sessions? - - - - - - - - - - - - ☐ ☐
- Do you know others who would be interested in this service? - - - - - ☐ ☐

What's the Plan?

You started your dog-walking business. After a few weeks, and only a few customers, you panic. You haven't made back the money you spent! Look back. Did you make a business plan? A business plan tells what product or service will be sold and how it will be sold. It tells who the customers will be, how much it will cost to start the business, how much it will cost to run the business, and what the profits are expected to be.

Figuring It All Out

You'll also need a budget to work out the financial details of your business. You need to know how many dogs you are going to walk each week and how much to charge each customer. You need to consider how much you are going to spend on advertising. In addition to all these items are your **start-up costs**. Most of these are one-time purchases, such as dog leashes, made before you open your business.

Word Bank

start-up costs *money spent to begin a business*

competition *other businesses selling a similar product*

Sharing the Spotlight

Suppose a friend decides to go into the dog-walking business in your neighborhood, too. You now have **competition**. When you start a business, you have to think about competition. Are there already businesses selling what you want to sell? Where are they? What are their products or services and their prices like? You may have to change your plan altogether.

A Matter of Fact

You might think that a new ice-cream company might not be very successful with all the competition around. Well, with a $12,000 investment ($4,000 of it borrowed), Ben Cohen and Jerry Greenfield opened an ice-cream shop in a renovated gas station in Burlington, Vermont. In 1997, Ben & Jerry's ice cream was sold worldwide, and the company was making a profit of about $6 million a year!

Putting in the Time— and the Money

The market survey is done, the business plan is finished, and you've prepared a budget. But there's still more work to do! You need to contact new customers and make schedules. And you have to actually start walking some dogs! Starting a business is a big **investment**. You may even need to borrow money or have other people invest in your business. This means that they give you money in the hope that when your business is successful they will get back more money than they invested. Starting a business is a risk, and it's hard work. But just imagine if it's a success!

Keeping Tabs on Your Business

Once your business is off and running, you'll want to check to see how it's doing. You'll need to see if you are making a profit or experiencing a **loss**. If your expenses for walking the dogs are more than the money the business has taken in, you'll have a loss. If you have money left over after your business expenses are paid, you've made a profit and can consider yourself a successful entrepreneur!

Business Smarts

Why do some businesses succeed while others fail? Sometimes a business fails due to poor planning or poor management. Sometimes there are other factors. Many people would agree that the secret of success lies not in having the right answers, but rather in asking the right questions, such as *Do people want to buy what I want to sell? Is there any competition for my business? How can I make my business more attractive to customers? Do I have enough money to start the business? How long can I wait before I need to start making a profit?*

A Penny for Your Thoughts

Imagine that there's room for another business in your neighborhood. What kind of business should it be? Ask yourself the questions on the left and find out if you think your business idea would be successful. You might even try to start it up!

Word Bank

investment *the risking of money and time to get something in return*

loss *the money a business loses when the cost of producing its goods and services is greater than the cost of selling them*

Supply and Demand

Is the Price Right?

Ever wonder why certain things cost more than others? It's true that store owners set the prices of their merchandise. But consumers also help determine prices. It's all a matter of **supply** and **demand**—that is, how much people want something and how much of that thing is available. If the demand is greater than the supply, the price goes up. If the supply is greater than the demand, the price goes down. Let's see how that works. Imagine you open a lemonade stand on a cloudy day. You start selling lemonade for 25¢ a glass. You get some customers—not too many, not too few—just enough to make a small profit. Then, the clouds disappear, the sun comes out, and it gets really hot. Now everybody's thirsty! They get in line at your stand. You decide that you can increase your profit if you raise the price to 30¢ a glass. Then you can afford a nicer lemonade stand! People want lemonade because it's hot, so they're willing to pay more. But watch out. If you raise the price too high, people might not want to buy your lemonade at all. What would you pay for a glass of lemonade on a hot day?

A Penny for Your Thoughts

Why do you think people are willing to pay higher prices for diamonds than for water, even though water is a necessity and diamonds aren't?

Not Enough to Go Around

Suppose there are so many people who want lemonade that you don't have enough to go around. Now there is a shortage of lemonade—there are more people who want lemonade than there is lemonade available. You have to go back and forth to the supermarket to buy more ingredients, and that uses up time you could be selling lemonade. You're losing money! You could hire somebody to help you, but that would cost money, too. You think about raising the price to make up the additional costs. If you do, you may be able to make a profit again.

Word Bank

supply *the amount of a good or service that is available to consumers*

demand *the desire of consumers for a good or service*

84

Too Much of a Good Thing

All of a sudden, there's a flash of lightning, a clap of thunder, and within five minutes, it's pouring rain. Suddenly, nobody wants lemonade, because they're running to get out of the rain. There is now a surplus of lemonade. This means that there is more lemonade available than you need for the people who want to buy it. There is a greater supply than demand. You have to lower your price to 10¢ a glass to get anybody to buy some. You hope to at least cover your costs, and you cross your fingers that it won't rain tomorrow! How do you think a lemonade stand would do in a place where it rained a lot?

Making Connections

Did you know that what happens in one part of the marketplace often affects what happens in another? For example, suppose the price of pay TV keeps going down and you could watch any movie at any time. Fewer people might actually go out to the movies. Some theaters might close. What would happen to all that uneaten popcorn? A decreased demand for popcorn at movie theaters could cause a decrease in its price.

Feeling Well—
A Healthy Economy

How do you know if a business is doing well? If there are profits, of course! But an economy doesn't make a profit, so how do you know if the economy is doing well? **Economists**, or people who study the economy, look at lots of different information to see if the economy is healthy. These include the prices of goods and services—whether they are rising or falling—and how many people are out of work or **unemployed**.

Looking for Work?

If you're over 16 and working or looking for work, you're considered part of the nation's work force. But if you're retired or under age 16, you're not counted as part of the work force—even if you do have a job.

The number of unemployed people is very important to the economy. If **unemployment** is low, most people who want a job have one, which usually means the economy is strong. But if the economy is weak, there are fewer jobs so more people have trouble earning money. What happens when unemployment is high? If you said fewer people buy and produce things, you're right.

Word Bank

economist *a person who studies the economy*

unemployed *being without a job, but looking for one*

unemployment *the total number of people out of work*

86 **savings rate** *the percent of income that people save*

Savings Rate!

Did you know that saving money can help the economy? For businesses to grow, they need to buy machines, buildings, and other materials. To do this, businesses usually borrow from banks. For money to be available for businesses to borrow, people must deposit savings into their bank accounts. So the **savings rate**—the percent of income that people save—can also tell you about the health of the economy.

A Penny for Your Thoughts

Did you know that the United States' savings rate has decline during the 1980s and 1990s? What do you think Americans are doing with their money instead of saving it?

Economy

Too Much Money?

Would you like to have more money to spend or save? Wouldn't it be great if everyone had more money? It sounds good, but the answer is actually no. When a lot of money is in circulation, **inflation** can occur. When things you buy, either goods or services, cost more than they used to, that's inflation. The prices have increased or inflated. Inflation is another measure of the economy because it shows how well the supply of goods and services in the country are meeting the demand of consumers like you.

Deflating Inflation

Remember how supply and demand affected the lemonade business? The national economy works the same way. If the supply of goods and services is equal to demand, there is little or no inflation. Goods and services cost about the same from year to year. But when there are increases in demand or costs of production go up, prices usually rise.

An increase in demand can be caused by lots of things, including more money in circulation. Why do you think an increase in the money supply increases demand? (Hint: An increase in the money supply means that people have more money and want to spend more on goods and services.)

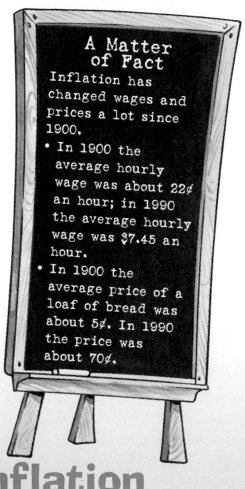

A Matter of Fact

Inflation has changed wages and prices a lot since 1900.

- In 1900 the average hourly wage was about 22¢ an hour; in 1990 the average hourly wage was $7.45 an hour.
- In 1900 the average price of a loaf of bread was about 5¢. In 1990 the price was about 70¢.

Inflation Hurts

Inflation can be hard on people. The value of money goes down during times of inflation. What you buy for a dollar today might cost two dollars tomorrow. This means your money is worth less than it was because it takes twice as much money to buy the same things. In general, many people find that their incomes don't rise as fast as prices.

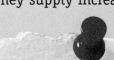

Word Bank

inflation *an economic condition characterized by rising prices*

A recession is when the economy stumbles.

A depression is when the economy trips and falls over!

Downturn or Disaster?

Suppose you're saving to buy a bicycle, but the price of the bicycle is rising faster than you can save. You might decide not to buy the bicycle. What if the same thing happens all across the country? If wages don't increase to keep up with the rising prices, people have less money to spend and products remain unsold. This causes manufacturers to produce fewer products. This leads to a cutback in workers and a rise in unemployment. All of this may cause a **recession**, a short time (two years or less) when the amount of business decreases.

A Penny for Your Thoughts

How well do you think your town's economy is doing? Are prices rising or falling? Are there a lot of jobs available? How can you tell?

Word Bank

recession *a period of time when the demand for goods declines, unemployment rises, and the flow of money slows down*

depression *a period of serious recession marked by high unemployment and a decline in business*

Oh No! A Depression!

Remember when you had a lot of lemonade and no buyers? What do you think would happen if this lasted a long time? Eventually a recession can turn into a **depression**, a time when there are too many goods and services and too little money to buy them. As a result, factories stop producing and shut down. Many people lose their jobs. They have less money or no money to spend. More goods are unsold, more factories close, and more workers are put out of work.

During a depression, prices decline. When there are too many goods for sale, people will sell them for less money rather than not sell them at all. Something that normally costs a dollar may cost only 50 cents. Also, people are willing to work for less money—just to have a job. So it costs less to produce goods.

Depositors waiting for their bank to open, 1930

The Great Depression

The Great Depression began in 1929 and lasted for ten years. In the United States, almost one third of all workers—about 15 million people—were out of work. Some people lost hope that economic conditions would improve, so they withdrew their money from the banks. So many people demanded their money at the same time that the banks couldn't meet their demands. The banks failed and had to close their doors. Millions of people lost their life savings. During the Great Depression 11,000 of the 25,000 banks in the United States closed.

Small Steps Back to Health

How did the United States economy recover? The American people looked to the federal government for help. Measures taken by Presidents Herbert Hoover and Franklin D. Roosevelt restored faith in the economy and provided relief for unemployed workers. Under Roosevelt's New Deal program, the government established the Public Works Administration, which created many new government jobs. As more people became employed, incomes increased and the demand for consumer goods rose as well.

Healthy at Last!

These programs were not enough to end depression conditions completely. The economy did not fully recover until World War II (1941–1945). The war created a demand for workers to not only replace soldiers who were overseas, but to produce the extra food and equipment for the troops. Finally, business improved. The period of **expansion** that everyone had hoped for had arrived.

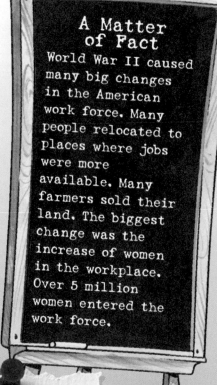

A Matter of Fact

World War II caused many big changes in the American work force. Many people relocated to places where jobs were more available. Many farmers sold their land. The biggest change was the increase of women in the workplace. Over 5 million women entered the work force.

Word Bank

expansion *a period of time during which the amount of business increases*

89

Take Your Pick!

When Rare Is Well-done!

Old penny stamps are very rare. Today they are worth between $250 and $5,000 each. Ancient coins are very rare, too. People are sometimes willing to pay thousands of dollars for a single silver coin. Why do some things increase in value as they become more scarce? Interview someone who has a stamp or coin collection, and find out what he or she thinks.

The Ups and Downs of Buying Shoes

In January, a new line of sandals came out. In March the price of a pair of the sandals went up $5, as people got ready for warm weather. In July the price rose until the sandals cost twice as much as they did in January. In September the price dropped $8, as summer ended. The September price was $30. How much did the sandals cost in January, March, and July?

A Mower or a Washer?

You're thinking of starting either a lawn-mowing business or a car-washing business. Which one do you think has greater start-up costs? Which one has greater day-to-day expenses? Which one would you rather do?

Chapter 8 The Government and Money

Why does the government **need** money? **How** does the government **get** money?

By now, you've probably had experience managing your own money. In this chapter you'll learn how the government manages the country's money.

What is the Federal Reserve System and why do we have it?
What are taxes?
How are our taxes spent?
Why does the government borrow money?

You'll find out a lot about the government and money. You'll see how the Federal Reserve protects the nation's economy. You'll learn about taxes—who pays them and why. You'll learn something about trade around the world. And you'll learn how all this affects you. You're a part of the big picture, and you have a role to play!

Who's in **Charge?**

The United States is a big country. The American government spends a great deal of money to run the country. So who manages the government's money? It's not the President, it's the Fed! The Federal Reserve System is the government's bank. It is divided into 12 regional banks across the country, with its main headquarters in Washington, D.C. The Fed's main work is to control the amount of money in circulation. It holds a percentage of the deposits of commercial banks and lends money to them when they really need it.

The Federal Reserve is the watchdog of the banking industry. Officials from the Fed regularly check banks' records to make sure they are following banking regulations.

Watchdog — now he's talking my language!

A Matter of Fact

The Fed is managed by the Federal Reserve Board of Governors—seven people who are chosen by the President and confirmed by the Senate. Each person serves one term of 14 years.

What Does the **Fed** Do?

- controls the amount of money in circulation
- regulates and supervises banks and banking practices
- administers federal consumer credit protection laws, which protect consumers who want credit
- makes sure that there is enough coin and paper money to meet public demand
- handles the government's checking accounts
- buys and sells dollars on foreign exchange markets (You'll learn more about the foreign exchange in the next chapter.)
- processes millions of checks that pass between banks every day

the Head

Controlling the Flow

How does the Fed control the amount of money in circulation? It acts like a traffic cop. When the Fed sees there is too much traffic, or money in the economy, it slows the economy down. The Fed can require banks to put more money in **reserve**—that's money that cannot be loaned. Or the Fed can cause banks to raise the interest rates on loans to customers. The more interest the banks charge, the fewer people want to borrow money. People have less to spend, so the amount of money in circulation decreases.

When there is not enough money in circulation, the Fed allows banks to keep less money in reserve. The banks then have more money to lend and can lower their interest rates to encourage customers to borrow money.

Word Bank

reserve *money that is kept in the bank and not loaned to bank customers*

Too Many Dollars

With more money in circulation, people spend more. Businesses expand and hire more people. But sometimes businesses can't produce all the things people want to buy. What happens? Prices may rise. On the other hand, if there isn't enough money in circulation, people won't spend very much. Businesses will not grow, and jobs will be harder to find. It's the Fed's job to keep spending in balance with the production of goods and services. It's quite a balancing act!

Weighing gold at the FRBNY vault

A Penny for Your Thoughts

Suppose prices of goods and services start rising. Would the Fed make credit more or less available? Why?

The Big Guy

The Federal Reserve Bank of New York (FRBNY) is the largest of the 12 Federal Reserve banks. The building has concrete walls 18 feet thick. It also has the largest currency vault in the world and holds 13,000 tons of gold! It is run mostly by computers and robotic devices. These computers and robots work 16 hours a day sorting and counting money. Altogether, the vault processes $2.7 billion a year!

Chipping In by Paying Taxes

Imagine walking down a street. You might see roads, trees, police officers, fire hydrants, schools, garbage cans, and libraries. Did you know that people help pay for all these things? No kidding! People help by paying taxes to city, state, and federal governments. A **tax** is money that a government collects from people and businesses. The government uses taxes to pay for the services it provides, such as schools, libraries, some hospitals, roads and bridges, and the armed forces.

A Penny for Your Thoughts

In France, in the 1600s, more than half of the tax money collected was spent collecting taxes. The cost of collecting taxes in the United States today is 1 percent of the money collected. Why does collecting taxes cost money?

A Pack of Taxes

The government collects taxes in lots of ways. You may pay taxes when you buy certain goods, like books and sports equipment. Adults pay taxes on the money that they earn from their jobs. Companies pay taxes on the profits that they make. People who own buildings pay taxes on the property that the buildings are on. If you inherit money or win the lottery, you pay taxes on what you receive. All the money collected in taxes pays for things that benefit everybody.

How Much Is Just Right?

How does the government decide how much tax people should pay? The government looks at two things: how much money it needs and how much people can afford. The government makes a budget to know how much money it will need to run the country. Then the government must decide how much of this money can be collected in taxes. If the government sets taxes too high, people may have less money to spend. If the government sets taxes too low, it won't be able to take in enough money to meet its expenses. When you're dealing with a multibillion-dollar budget, it can get a bit tricky!

Did you know your family probably pays more in taxes than it spends on food and clothing combined?

Tax-ing!

Just a Little Bit More

Think about the last time you bought something. You looked at the price tag and thought "Oh, I have to pay that much." But when you got to the counter, the item might have cost a little bit more! That's because you probably paid sales tax on your purchase. **Sales tax** is a **surcharge**, or extra charge, that's sometimes added to specific items, such as clothing and electronic equipment. So suppose you're saving up for a particular item, like a bicycle. Don't forget to save for the sales tax!

Go Figure!

Did you know that you pay more sales tax on a bicycle than you do on a notebook? That's because sales tax is a percent of the total cost of the item. The more an item costs, the greater the sales tax.

Here's how to figure sales tax.

- Find out what the sales tax is in your state. The figure will be a percent, such as 6 percent.

- Change the percent to a decimal. (For example, 6 percent is .06, and 8½ percent is .085.)

- Then multiply that number by the price of the item.

- The product is the correct sales tax. Round off to the nearest penny, if necessary.

- Add the sales tax to the price of the item to get the total amount you have to pay.

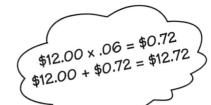

Word Bank

tax *money that one must pay to help support a government*

sales tax *a tax on sales and some services that is usually added to the price by the seller*

surcharge *an extra cost added to an original cost*

Putting Your Two Cents In

Did you know that every February, March, and April, adults all over the country are filling out forms? These forms are for their **income tax**, which is a tax that people and businesses pay yearly. Most people pay income tax to state and federal governments. The amount of income tax that people pay is based on their **earned income**—the income they receive through their jobs—and their **unearned income**, such as interest from a savings account and money earned from other investments. Income tax is paid on a certain percent of your income. People who earn more money usually have to pay more taxes than those who earn less. The amount of income tax that people pay also depends on whether they have other people to support, such as children. Do you think the system is fair?

Word Bank

income tax *a tax on a person's income*

earned income *money received from jobs*

unearned income *money received from investments such as savings accounts and bonds*

How Much Would You Pay?

Do you earn any money? If it's less than $4,000 a year, you don't have to pay income tax. But suppose you had a full-time job. How much you earn determines the percent you have to pay. Look at the chart and you'll see!

Federal Income Tax for a Single Person, 1997

If Income Is	Percent Taken Out
less than $24,000	15%
$24,000 to $58,150	28%
$58,150 to $121,300	31%
$121,300 to $263,750	36%
more than $263,750	39.6%

A Do-It-Yourself Income Tax

What do you think about having a family income tax? Here's how it would work. Each member of the family must contribute a percent of his or her total income or allowance weekly into a large jar or container—known as the tax jar. At the end of the year, decide together what to do with the money. Will you put it toward a family trip? Will you go out for dinner? Will you buy a computer game?

Who Pays Taxes?

Is everybody chipping in? Yes, everyone who lives and works in the United States must pay income taxes. But there are a few exceptions. For instance, people who visit the United States from other countries and stay and work for a short time do not pay income tax. These individuals are **tax-exempt**, which means they do not have to pay taxes on their income.

Like individuals, certain organizations are tax-exempt. **Nonprofit** groups, such as colleges, churches, and charitable organizations, are excused from paying taxes. A nonprofit organization is one that uses all the money it makes to cover its expenses and to further its goals. For instance, a religious institution such as a church uses the money it makes to pay for its programs and employees and to create more programs.

A Penny for Your Thoughts
Can you think of any ideas for a nonprofit organization? Are there any causes that you would like to work on? Do you know of any nonprofit organizations that work for that cause?

Looking to the Future

Ever wonder how people pay for things after they retire? In addition to retirement savings, investments, or other income, many people receive **Social Security** benefits. Social Security is a federal system of financial support for retired workers and people who are unable to work because of a disability. Workers pay into the system by having Social Security taxes deducted from their pay. Employers are also required to pay taxes to Social Security for each employee. At retirement, a worker will receive a monthly check to use as a source of income. It's like having a savings account with the federal government.

Word Bank

tax-exempt *excused from paying taxes*

nonprofit *not intending to make a profit*

Social Security *a system of government financial support for those who are retired or unable to work*

When Taxes Aren't Enough

What do you do when you need something right away but don't have the money to pay for it? You might borrow money from your family or from a friend. When the federal or state government needs money, it does the same thing—it borrows money! But the government doesn't go to the bank to get a loan. Instead it sells certificates called **bonds**. A bond is like a loan to the government or any large company. And just like a bank loan, the borrower must pay interest to the lender. And who is the lender? It could be you! Is buying government bonds a safe investment? Yes! If the government doesn't have enough money to pay off its bonds, it can issue new bonds or raise taxes.

It's a Bond-ing Experience

Though the government issues many different bonds, the most common ones are savings bonds. Where do you get them? What do they cost? You can buy a savings bond at most banks or from a Federal Reserve bank. Your cost or investment is half the face value. That means if you buy a $50 bond, it will cost you $25. It will be worth the face value or $50 when the bond **matures**, which could be in 10 years. But you can cash in the bond at any time after 6 months. Just remember, the longer you hold a bond, the more interest it earns.

To Mary Ann Gonet
Box 99
Anytown, Anystate 01234

A Matter of Fact

The government issues several different types of savings bonds. They may be bought in denominations of $50, $100, $500, $1,000, $5,000, and $10,000.

Word Bank

bond *a certificate of a loan to a government or business*
mature *able to be redeemed for the face value*

Borrows Money

Government Overspending

Do you owe anybody any money? If you do, you and the federal government have something in common. Over the years, the federal government has spent a lot of money. It has also run up a huge debt. The **national debt** is more than $5 trillion ($5,000,000,000,000). Now that's a lot of zeros! If this debt were divided among every man, woman, and child in the United States, each person would owe about $20,000. How did the government build up so much debt? As you can see from the chart, it took a lot of time. Often the cost of war causes a big increase in the national debt. It all started when the government took over $75 million in debts accumulated from the Revolutionary War.

The interest owed on the national debt is over $300,000,000!

That's going to keep everybody interest-ed for a long time! That's more than $821,917 a day!

We've Got a Big Debt

What happens if you owe a lot of money to a lot of people? For one thing, you have to work extra hard to pay off the debt. If everybody that you owe money to wanted it at one time, you'd be in a jam. Also, if you owe too much money, people may stop lending you money. What about the government's debt? To pay off the debt, the government might raise taxes. When taxes are raised, people have less money to spend. Less money spent means less business growth and fewer new jobs. And it's possible that if the debt continues to grow, people may stop lending money to the government.

National Debt

Year	Amount of Debt
1800	$82,976,294
1825	$83,788,433
1850	$63,452,774
1875	$2,232,284,532
1900	$2,136,961,091
1925	$20,516,193,888
1950	$257,357,352,351
1975	$576,649,000,000*
1995	$4,921,018,000,000*

*Rounded to millions

Word Bank
national debt *the amount of money the government owes*

99

Money Makes the
World Go Round

When you buy something at the supermarket, what do you use? Dollars and cents of course! You may pay with cash, credit cards, or checks, but it's still in dollars and cents. The dollar is the main unit of currency in the United States. If everyone in the world used the same currency, life would be simple. But each country has its own money. In fact, there are approximately 140 different currencies in the world today.

Import or Export?

What kinds of products are made where you live? Every country produces different types of products. One country must trade with another to get products that are not produced within its own country. Goods that are brought into a country for sale from other countries are called **imports**. Goods that a country sends to other countries for sale are called **exports**. What goods are imported into the United States? Can you think of any goods that we export?

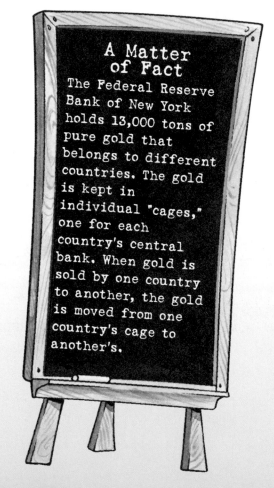

A Matter of Fact

The Federal Reserve Bank of New York holds 13,000 tons of pure gold that belongs to different countries. The gold is kept in individual "cages," one for each country's central bank. When gold is sold by one country to another, the gold is moved from one country's cage to another's.

A Dollar, A Pound

If you visit another country and buy something, you usually have to pay for the item with that country's money. To do this, you would exchange your money for the currency of the country you are in. But the value of currency in each country might be different. For instance, one British pound may be worth two American dollars. If this were true, which would you rather have, one pound or one dollar?

Word Bank

import *goods that are brought into one country from another*

export *goods that are sent from one country to another*

Currency Exchange Board

		We Sell At	We Buy At
CANADA	CAD		
UNITED KINGDOM	GBP		
JAPAN	YEN		
SWITZERLAND	SFR		
FRANCE	FRF		
W. GERMANY	DEM		
AUSTRALIA	A$		
SPAIN	PTS		
ITALY	LIRE		

The Foreign Exchange Market

How do you think the value of currencies are agreed upon? How much a currency is worth compared to another currency, called the **exchange rate**, is determined at the **foreign exchange market**. This is the place where foreign exchange dealers in major cities like New York, London, Tokyo, and Paris trade the money of different countries.

How Does It Work?

How are exchange rates determined? They are based on supply and demand. For example, if Americans want to buy Japanese goods, they need Japanese money, or yen, to pay for the goods. This creates a demand for the yen, so the value of the yen goes up. When the value of the yen goes up, Japanese goods become more expensive. If the goods become too expensive, people will buy fewer Japanese goods. Then the value of the yen will fall. And people will be able to get more yen for a dollar.

A Test of Strength

Did you know that the dollar can be weak or strong? When the dollar has a high value in comparison with the currencies of other countries, it is considered strong. This happens when there is a large demand for American goods. On the other hand, when the demand for American goods and services is low, the dollar is weak—it has a low value compared with the currencies of other countries. When you travel abroad, you will be able to buy more with your money if the dollar is strong.

Word Bank

exchange rate *the value of one nation's currency in comparison to another*

foreign exchange market *the place where foreign exchange dealers in major cities around the world trade the money of different countries*

A Penny for Your Thoughts

Suppose you have a choice between something made in America or something that has been imported. What are some reasons you might choose one over the other?

Take Your Pick!

Taxing Questions

If there were no taxes, would there be public schools? Is there anything else that would be missing from your community if there were no taxes? Suppose your state wanted to build a bridge. How could it get the money?

Buy Time

You just received $35 for your birthday. You want to buy a new jacket for $32.99, but the sales tax is 8 percent. Do you have enough money?

Currency Exchange Rates

Where can you get the best buy? Suppose the same bicycle costs 200 American dollars, 130 British pounds, 417 German marks, and 22,542 Japanese yen. Look in the newspaper to find the current exchange rates for these currencies. Where can you get the best deal?

It's Import-ant!

Are you wearing an import? Perhaps your shoes were made in another country. How do you think they got to your feet? Make up a story describing "The Great Traveling Shoes."

Chapter 9

Investing
Money

Why should I **invest?**
What are my **options?**

You've learned the importance of saving money and spending it wisely. In this chapter, you will learn that sometimes you can really make the money you save grow.

What are stocks and bonds?
What's so great about the stock market?
What does it mean to invest money wisely?

This chapter will help you understand the ins and outs of owning stock. You'll learn how the stock market works. You'll understand the difference between stocks and bonds. You'll learn that there are different ways to invest your money. When it comes to money, you won't be green anymore!

103

Stocking Up

It's in Stock!

Suppose you own a small business, such as a lawn-mowing service. But you don't have enough money to buy the new lawn mower you need. What could you do to get more money? You could borrow money or you could invite friends to share in the cost of your business—for a profit of course.

This is similar to what companies do when they need money to expand or grow. They sell stock. **Stocks** are like bricks in a building. If you own a brick, you own a **share**, or part of the building. Owning a stock means that you are a **stockholder** or a **shareholder**—a part owner of the company. So you own a share of everything the company owns.

Opening Up to Stockholders

When the owners of a company decide they want to sell stock in their company, they "go public." This means they sell shares to anyone who wants to buy them. How many shares do they sell? It's up to the owners of the company. It could be one hundred, one thousand, one million, or more.

A Penny for Your Thoughts

If you owned shares in a company that made cars, what might you want the company to focus on? New models, cutting costs, new technology?

Having a Say in the Company

Congratulations! You've bought stock! When you hold stock in a company, you can have a say in how the company is run. Every year, shareholders are invited to an annual shareholders' meeting. At the meeting they may vote on certain future company plans. Every share is worth one vote. As you might have guessed, the more shares a person has, the more power he or she has in company decision-making.

Word Bank

stock *a part of a company that may be purchased by the public*

share *a part of a company that may be bought by someone as an investment*

stockholder or shareholder *a person who owns stock or shares in a company*

A stock certificate

n Stocks

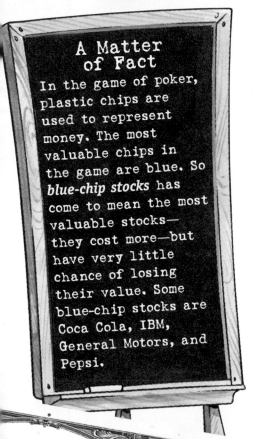

A Matter of Fact

In the game of poker, plastic chips are used to represent money. The most valuable chips in the game are blue. So *blue-chip stocks* has come to mean the most valuable stocks— they cost more—but have very little chance of losing their value. Some blue-chip stocks are Coca Cola, IBM, General Motors, and Pepsi.

It Can Be Good to Stock Up

Why do people buy stock? To make money! You want your stock to be worth more than what you paid. If the company does well, you can expect the value of your shares to go up. If you decided to sell your shares, you would receive more money than you paid. You can hold onto your shares for as long as you want. You choose when you want to sell them. You may also receive **dividends**, which are part of the company's profits. Some of the profits are divided among the stockholders, who usually receive dividends every three months.

Good Times and Bad

What happens if the company that you own stock in has a loss? The value of your shares would probably go down. Investing in stocks can be tricky! As part owner of the company, you must take the good times with the bad. There is always the risk that the value of the shares you buy will go down. It is possible that the value of your shares can go down so far that you lose the money you invested in the company. So before you buy stock in a company, you should do some research. What does the company do? How long has it been around? Has it been successful?

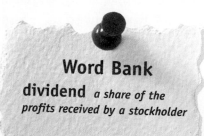

Word Bank
dividend *a share of the profits received by a stockholder*

ACOM

ACOM INC.
THE LAWS OF THE STATE OF DELAWARE

CUSIP 925524 30 8
SEE REVERSE FOR CERTAIN DEFINITIONS

RES OF THE CLASS B COMMON STOCK OF

The Supermarket

Who's Selling?

You've done your research, and you've decided to invest some money in a particular company. Where do you go? When you want to buy or sell stocks, you contact a **stockbroker,** a person who buys and sells shares of stock for customers. Stockbrokers are paid **commissions**, or fees, on the stocks they buy and sell. A commission is usually a percent of the total cost of the stocks bought or sold.

This is Some Market!

If you ever listen to news reports on TV or radio, you might have heard about stocks rising and falling. What does that mean? The prices are going up or going down. Prices of stocks are determined by the **stock market**, where they are bought and sold. Stock prices may change daily. The stock market is like a supermarket for buying and selling shares in different companies. If there are many people who want to buy a share in a company, the price of the shares will go up. If there are many people who want to sell shares in a company, the price will go down.

The Big Board

The United States stock market is made up of several different stock exchanges or stock markets. The three main ones are the New York Stock Exchange (NYSE), the National Association of Securities Dealers Automated Quotations (NASDAQ) exchange, and the American Stock Exchange (AMEX). NYSE and AMEX are located in New York City. But NASDAQ is actually a system of computers that are networked, or linked together.

Did you know that 51 million Americans own stock?

A Penny for Your Thoughts

Do you think buying stocks is a good investment? Would you rather buy stock or keep your money in a savings account? Why?

Word Bank

stockbroker *a person who buys and sells shares of stock for other people*

commission *the fee paid to a stockbroker for buying or selling stocks*

stock market *a place where shares of many different companies are bought and sold*

# of Stocks

If you've ever seen stockbrokers in action, buying and selling stocks at the New York Stock Exchange, you'd think you were in the middle of a giant rush-hour traffic jam. The place is crowded and noisy. People rush back and forth. It's quite different from the early days of the NYSE. In 1792, 24 brokers and merchants met under a tree on Wall Street in New York City.

Bulls and Bears

At the original New York Stock Exchange, people put notes on a bulletin board when they wanted to buy or sell stocks. When the market was doing well, there were many notes or "bulletins" on the board. When the market wasn't doing well, the board was bare. Today a market in which stocks are rising is called a **bull market**. "Bulls" are people who expect stock prices to rise. A market in which stock prices are falling is called a **bear market**. "Bears" are people who expect stock prices to drop. Is today's market bullish or bearish? Look in the newspaper or listen to the news to find out!

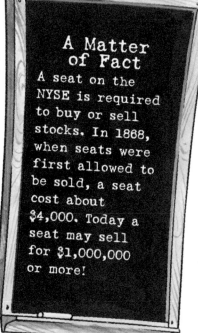

A Matter of Fact
A seat on the NYSE is required to buy or sell stocks. In 1868, when seats were first allowed to be sold, a seat cost about $4,000. Today a seat may sell for $1,000,000 or more!

The New York Stock Exchange

Word Bank
bull market *a period in which the stock market does well and prices are up*

bear market *a period in which the stock market does poorly and prices go down*

Boning Up on the Stock Market

Suppose you saved up some money and bought 10 shares of Reebok stock. The value of your stock may change every day. Your stock may go up while other stocks are going down. To find out the value of your stock, turn to the business section of a newspaper or search the Internet to find the stock report or quote. A stock report looks much more complicated than it actually is. Here's a close-up of one from a newspaper.

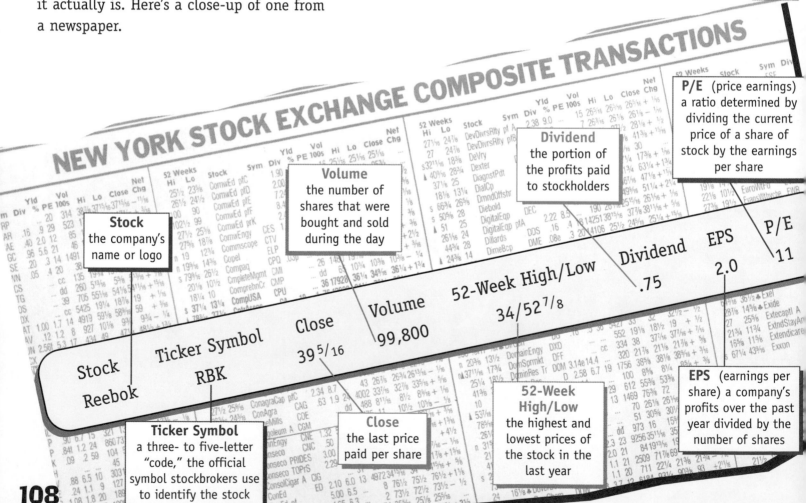

NEW YORK STOCK EXCHANGE COMPOSITE TRANSACTIONS

Stock
the company's name or logo

Volume
the number of shares that were bought and sold during the day

Dividend
the portion of the profits paid to stockholders

P/E (price earnings) a ratio determined by dividing the current price of a share of stock by the earnings per share

Stock	Ticker Symbol	Close	Volume	52-Week High/Low	Dividend	EPS	P/E
Reebok	RBK	39 5/16	99,800	34/52 7/8	.75	2.0	11

Ticker Symbol
a three- to five-letter "code," the official symbol stockbrokers use to identify the stock

Close
the last price paid per share

52-Week High/Low
the highest and lowest prices of the stock in the last year

EPS (earnings per share) a company's profits over the past year divided by the number of shares

A Penny for Your Thoughts
What kind of things would you look for in a stock investment?

Winning on Wall Street

Is there any way to really know if stocks will go up or down? Not really. The best advice about choosing stocks, however, is to follow three simple steps.

STEP 1 Buy stock in a company you know something about. We all have to eat and take medicine, even when there may be less money than usual to spend. Food and drug stocks, therefore, are safe bets since they tend to hold their prices even during troubled times. Other industries that remain pretty steady are gas, water, electric, and phone companies.

STEP 2 Research a few companies. Call a brokerage firm and ask for information on the companies you've chosen. Follow the stocks' prices in the newspaper or on-line. Call the companies and ask for their annual reports.

STEP 3 Know your investment goals. Do you want your money to grow to meet a future need, such as college? Or do you want income to spend right now? How much risk are you willing to take? Identifying your goals will help you determine which stock to buy.

So Who Is This Guy?

Have you ever heard of Dow Jones? Dow Jones & Company is a financial news publisher that researches the stock market. This research is used by investors to help predict when stocks will increase or decrease in value. The **Dow Jones Industrial Average**, also called the Dow, is a number that indicates the average of closing prices of 30 selected stocks. These stocks are chosen because their performance is a good indicator of how the stock market is doing overall. If the Dow is rising, the rest of the stock market is generally rising, too. Take a look in the newspaper. Did the Dow rise or fall yesterday?

Word Bank
Dow Jones Industrial Average (DJIA)
a number indicating the average closing prices of the 30 industrial stocks; also called the Dow

So Many Ways to Invest

Have you ever looked in the financial section of the newspaper or listened to the financial news on TV? There's a lot more to the world of big business than stocks. You have many options, or choices for investing. Armed with that knowledge, one day you'll be ready to take on the world of investing!

These Bonds Don't Break

Remember, one way the government borrows money is by selling bonds. Well, companies can sell bonds, too. These bonds allow you to invest money for a fixed period of time at a fixed interest rate. You receive interest regularly until the bond matures. Once it does, you receive the principal back.

Is a fixed interest rate a good thing? It can be good or bad. Suppose that, after you buy a bond, the interest rates on new bonds change. If the bond you bought has an interest rate of 12 percent and interest rates on new bonds are lower, your bond becomes more valuable. If the interest rate on new bonds is higher, your bond becomes less valuable.

Stocks or Bonds?

What's the difference between stocks and bonds? When you buy stock, you are buying a share in a company. But when you buy bonds, you are just lending money to the company. You don't have a say in the way the company is run. And no matter how the company does, you still receive the same amount of interest.

A Penny for Your Thoughts

Would you rather buy stocks or bonds? Would you rather buy government bonds or company bonds?

Options?

Having a Fund Time

Suppose you bought several shares of stock from a few different companies. Your investments did well. Now your friends ask if you would invest some money for them. This is similar to how a **mutual fund** works. A mutual fund is a company that sells stock in itself to investors and then uses that money to invest in other companies. The fund is run by a professional manager. It is up to the professional, not the individual investors, to decide what to buy and sell. Since a mutual fund has a variety of different investments, its success does not depend on one particular stock or bond. Why might you invest in a mutual fund? Maybe you don't feel confident about buying stocks or bonds by yourself. Maybe you don't have the time or knowledge to follow the stock market and make informed choices. Also, the fact that the fund has many customers like yourself enables the fund to have more power in making investments.

There's Still More!

Did you know that there are many more ways to invest your money? You can buy real estate (houses, buildings, and land). You can buy precious gems and metals, such as diamonds and gold. You can invest in foreign currencies or in natural resources like oil. You can put money into small businesses that are just starting. You can invest money in your own small business! You have many options.

Word Bank
mutual fund *a company that sells stock in itself and then uses that money to invest in other companies*

111

Hey, Big Spender!

Suppose you had $5,000. What would you do with it?

When you save or invest money, you must think about how much risk you are willing to take. The safer your investment, the less money you are likely to earn. The riskier the investment, the greater the chance you have of losing your money or making a lot of money.

Each type of investment, from stocks to bonds to mutual funds, has a certain amount of risk. In general, the riskier an investment, the greater the possible profit. When you choose investments, you have to decide how much risk you want to take. The risk you are willing to take depends on what your goals are, your personality, and how much time and money you are willing to invest.

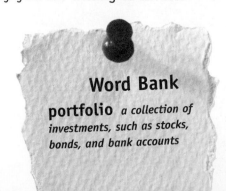

Word Bank

portfolio *a collection of investments, such as stocks, bonds, and bank accounts*

Keeping It in Mind

How should you weigh risk and return? First of all, you have to decide why you are investing. Do you want an income now, or are you saving for something further down the road? The longer the period you invest your money for, the less the ups and downs of the stock market will affect you. So the risk is less. You also have to decide how much risk you can handle. If you take a big risk with your money, will you spend lots of sleepless nights worrying if your investments are doing well? Everybody has a certain level of risk that they feel comfortable taking. You may want to make a lot of money, but if you're worrying all the time, the risk is probably not worth it.

Putting It All Together

Do you think you should put all your money into one investment? Many people invest their money in a variety of ways. They buy some stocks and some bonds and also deposit money in a bank account. Your **portfolio** consists of all the investment choices that you have made. The contents of your portfolio are up to you, depending on your needs and goals.

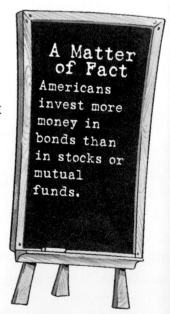

A Matter of Fact
Americans invest more money in bonds than in stocks or mutual funds.

Investment Choices

Each type of investment has its own level of risk. Which suits your needs best?

Bank accounts Bank accounts, like savings accounts, CDs, and money market accounts, have a very small amount of risk. But these accounts pay relatively low rates of interest.

Bonds Bonds are usually a safe investment. But be careful whose bonds you buy. Sometimes bonds that pay higher interest rates are riskier because the company that issued them may not be able to pay you when the bond is due. In general, government bonds are the safest.

Mutual funds The risk of investing in a mutual fund depends on the kinds of stocks and bonds it buys. For example, a mutual fund that invests in blue-chip stocks and bonds is much less risky than a mutual fund that invests in new technology stocks.

Stocks Buying individual stocks can be very rewarding but also very risky. You have to know what you're doing.

A Penny for Your Thoughts

So now you know something about investing money. What tips do you have to share with others? What are things to consider? What are things to avoid?

When the Payoff's Not Cash

You can put money to work for you in many ways. But money can also be shared with others to help those who are in need. How you choose to donate your time or money toward helping others is a personal matter. Some people donate money to support particular causes, such as protecting the environment. Others donate money to organizations like UNICEF, which helps needy children by providing food, medicine, and education programs. Understanding how to use money—to benefit yourself and others—is an important life skill. You now have a lot of the know-how in your pocket. How you choose to use it to build a productive and rewarding life is up to you.

113

Take Your Pick!

It's a Zoo!

Here are some terms that have to do with the stock market. Can you guess how they got their names?

cage—the room in the broker's office where cash and securities are handled

cash cow—a company that earns a lot of money

cats and dogs—poor-quality stocks

goldbugs—investors who think that buying gold is the best investment

turkey—a poor investment; a dud

Buy Low, Sell High

Keeping a Close Eye on Your Investments

Choose a stock to follow. It could be the company that makes your favorite sneakers, movies, toys, cereal—you name it! Check the newspaper's business section to see if the company is publicly traded on a stock exchange. Then you can see how "your company" is doing every day. Would your company be a good investment?

Buying stock is a cinch. You buy low and sell high. That means buy stock when the price is low and sell stock when the price is high.

If it were that easy, everybody would be rich!

Why do you think investing in stock is not as easy as she says it is?

Glossary

alloy   a mixture of two or more metals

ATM card   a bank card that allows customers to use an ATM machine

automated-teller machine (ATM)   a machine that performs most of the banking operations that a human teller can

balance   the amount of money in a bank account

balanced budget   a budget in which the money going out is equal to or less than the money taken in

bank   a business that keeps money for customers, makes loans, and provides other money-related services

bank statement   a monthly summary of a customer's bank transactions

barter   trading goods or services with someone for different goods or services, without using money

bear market   a period in which the stock market does poorly and prices go down

bond   a certificate of a loan to a government or a business

bounced check   a check returned by the bank for lack of funds

budget   a plan of how much money a person, business, government, or organization is able to spend and how it will be spent

bull market   a period in which the stock market does well and prices are up

business   an enterprise that brings in money from selling goods or services

cash   bills and coins, or to give or get cash for, as in to *cash* a check

cashier's check   a check guaranteed by the bank

check   a written order to a bank to pay a specified amount of money to a specified person or company, from money on deposit with the bank

circulation   money that is available for use

clearinghouse   a place where banks exchange checks and settle accounts

collateral   property, such as a house or car, that a borrower promises to give to the lender in case of a loan default

commission   the fee paid to a stockbroker for making a trade

comparison shopper   one who examines products to see how they are alike or different

competition   other businesses selling a similar product

consumer   someone who buys and uses good and services

continentals   paper money printed by Congress during the American Revolution

cosign   to sign a document for another person, indicating responsibility if the borrower defaults

counterfeit   to make a copy of something that people will think is genuine

credit   money loaned, usually for a fee, that must be paid back

credit card   a card that allows a person to make purchases on credit

credit limit   the amount of credit available to a person

credit terms   conditions of credit, such as interest rates and fees

currency   any kind of money that is used as a medium of exchange

debit card   a bank card that allows a person to withdraw money electronically from a checking account

debt   money owed when you buy something on credit or borrow money

default   to fail to repay a loan

demand   the desire of consumers for a good or service

denomination   bills of a particular value

deposit   the money put into a bank account

depression   a period of serious recession marked by high unemployment and a decline in business

direct deposit   having a check electronically deposited in a bank rather than receiving the check

dividend   a share of the profits received by a stockholder

dollar   the official unit of currency in the United States; based on the decimal system

donate   to contribute money, a gift, or time to a worthy cause, fund, or charity

Dow Jones Industrial Average (DJIA)   a number indicating the average closing prices of 30 selected stocks; also called the Dow

down payment   an amount of money paid as an initial lump sum payment for a debt

earned income   money received from jobs

economist   a person who studies the economy

economy   the way in which human resources and natural resources are used to produce goods and services

electronic funds transfer   moving money from one account to another via computer

electrum   a natural mixture of gold and silver

employee   a person who works for another in return for pay

employer   a person or company for whom other people work for pay

endorse   to sign your name on the back of a check

entrepreneur   a person who creates and manages a business

exchange rate   the value of one nation's currency in comparison to another

expansion   a period of time during which the amount of business increases

export   a good that is sent from one country to another; to send goods from one country for sale in another

Federal Reserve   the central bank of the United States

fee   money charged for a service

foreign exchange market   the place where foreign exchange dealers in major cities around the world trade the money of different countries

gold standard   the system of currency in which paper money can be exchanged for a fixed amount of gold

goods   real items, such as cars, wristwatches, and clothing

greenbacks   the first official paper money printed by the U.S. government

import   a good that is brought into one country from another; to bring goods into one country from another

income   the money a person gets from salary or wages, profits, interest, investments, and other sources

income tax   a tax on a person's income

inflation an economic condition characterized by rising prices

ingot   metal cast in a convenient shape before it is made into something else

installment   partial payment of a debt, paid regularly

interest   the money a person pays to borrow money, or the money a bank pays depositors for using their money

investment   the risking of money and time to get something in return

line of credit   an agreed-upon amount of money that can be borrowed from a bank

loan   a sum of money borrowed for a certain amount of time

loss   the money a business loses when the cost of producing its products is greater than the cost of selling them

market survey   a questionnaire designed to find out what people think about a particular product or service

mature   able to be redeemed

medium of exchange   anything that a group of people agree has a certain worth

milled coin   a coin with ridged edges

minimum balance   a fixed amount of money that remains in a customer's account to avoid paying bank fees

minimum deposit   the least amount of money required to open an account

mint   to stamp coins out of metal; a place where the coins of a country are made

money   anything a group of people accept in exchange for goods and services

money order   a written order, or check, that a sum of money be paid to a certain person or business

mortgage   a loan given to pay for a house or building

mutual fund   a company that sells stock in itself and then uses that money to invest in other companies

national debt   the amount of money that the government owes

natural resource   a supply of something that is found naturally on Earth

need   something that you must have

nonprofit   a business not intending to make a profit

opportunity cost   the cost of what you are giving up to get something you want more

pawnbroker   a person who lends money at a specified rate to people who leave items as security

pawnshop   a place to leave an item of value in exchange for a loan

PC banking   using a home or office computer to carry out bank transactions

personal identification number (PIN)   a code that activates an ATM card to allow purchases to be made

portfolio   a collection of investments, such as stocks, bonds, and bank accounts

precious metals   metals, such as gold and silver, that are valuable because they are rare

principal   a sum of money in an account, not including interest

private sector   the part of the economy produced by individuals and businesses

producer   the people or businesses that provide goods and services

profit   the money a business makes after expenses are paid

promissory note   a written promise to pay a sum of money

public sector   the part of the economy produced by the government

recession   a period of time when the demand for goods declines, unemployment rises, and the flow of money slows down

register   the part of a checkbook where transactions are recorded

reserve   money that is kept in a bank and not loaned to customers

retirement when a person gives up his or her job often because of age

risk the chance of loss

safe-deposit box a place to keep special items at a bank

salary a fixed amount of money paid regularly for work done, usually a yearly rate of pay

sales tax a tax on sales and some services that is usually added to the price by the seller

savings money that is put away to be used later

savings rate the percent of income that people save

services work that is done for other people; for example, work done by waiters, lawyers, and nurse

share a part of a company that can be bought by someone as an investment

Social Security a system of federal financial support for retired workers and workers unable to work because of a disability

start-up costs money spent to begin a business

stock a part of a company that may be purchased by the public

stockbroker a person who buys and sells stocks and bonds for other people

stockholder or shareholder a person who owns stock, or shares, in a company

stock market place where shares of many different companies are bought and sold

supply the amount of a good or service that is available to consumers

surcharge an extra cost added on to an original cost

taxes money that a government collects from people and businesses

tax-exempt not required to pay taxes

transaction any business done with the bank, such as a deposit or withdrawal

traveler's check a special kind of check used by travelers instead of cash

unearned income money received from investments such as savings accounts and bonds

unemployed being without a job but looking for one

unemployment the total number of people out of work

value the worth of something as measured in goods, services, or a medium of exchange

wages money paid to an employee for work done, may be an hourly rate of pay

Wall Street a street in New York City where major banks and companies conduct business; a symbol of the financial world

want something that you would like to have but don't necessarily need

warranty a written guarantee to repair or replace a product if something goes wrong within a limited period of time

welfare income paid by the government to people who need it to live

withdrawal taking money from a bank account

Index

answers

TAKE YOUR PICK ANSWERS

Page 16

Worth His Weight in Gold "All that glitters is not gold" means that just because something looks valuable doesn't necessarily mean it is.

Penny Power Move pennies as shown:

Coining Phrases a dime a dozen—very common; easy money—money made with very little effort; pocket money—a small amount of money; penny-wise and pound-foolish—cutting back on a cost only to have it cost more in the end; the buck stops here—assume responsibility for decisions; break the bank—cost more money than a person has; rolling in dough—rich

Weighty Question A pound of feathers weighs the same as a pound of gold.

Page 28

Make Your Moves 1. Slide the penny from box 2 to box 3. 2. Jump the nickel from box 4 to box 2. 3. Slide the nickel from box 5 to box 4. 4. Jump the penny from box 3 to box 5. 5. Jump the penny from box 1 to box 3. 6. Slide the nickel from box 2 to box 1. 7. Jump the nickel from box 4 to box 2. 8. Slide the penny from box 3 to box 4.

Naming Coins 2 dimes, 2 nickels, 1 quarter

In Mint Condition 451,000,000 pennies ÷ 100 = $4,510,000; 2,000,000 nickels ÷ 20 = $100,000; 10,000,000 dimes ÷ 10 = $1,000,000; 4,000,000 quarters ÷ 4 = $1,000,000; 120,000 half dollars ÷ 2 = $60,000; Total = $6,670,000 per day X 257 days per yr. = $1,714,190,000

Page 38

Shop 'Til You Drop 3,472 days

Page 52

Count on It! It would take about 525,000 X 12 = 6,300,000 days (approximately 17,500 years) to count to 525 billion.

You need to know the height of the Sears Tower. 525 billion dollar bills would stack to a height of 187,768,240 feet. Since the Sears Tower is 1,454 feet high, the stack of bills would be about 129,000 (187,768,240 ÷ 1,454 = 129,139) times as high as the building.

Deposits and Withdrawals The total amount of the three deposits was more than the one withdrawal.

Break the Bank $20/month; if you receive a penny the first day and have your salary doubled each successive day, you will earn a total of $163.83 in two weeks, and $10,737,418.23 in 30 days or $21,474,836.47 in 31 days.

Page 66

It's Your Money 5 weeks

Logical Savings Character 1: $8; Character 2: $5; Character 3: $16

It All Adds Up (Or Does It?) Never; each month you receive $5 in interest, and you take out $5, so your balance at the end of the month is always $100.

Page 76

Credit: Pro or Con? Advantages: good for emergencies; accepted all over the world; protection from theft; Disadvantages: spending what you can't afford; yearly fees; interest payments

Page 90

When Rare Is Well-Done! Generally the demand increases for items that are scarce when people decide they are valuable, causing the price of the items to go up.

The Ups and Downs of Buying Shoes January—$19; March—$24; July—$38

A Mower or a Washer? Start-up costs are probably greater for a lawn-mowing business because more expensive equipment is needed. A car-washing business may have higher day-to-day expenses depending on the cost of water. But a lawn mower might require the use of gas, which could be expensive.

Page 102

Taxing Questions Taxes pay for many things, such as public hospitals, libraries, and roads. A state could issue a bond to raise money needed for special projects.

Buy Time No; the total cost of the jacket is $33.63.

Page 114

Buy Low, Sell High Stocks are unpredictable. It is impossible to know when a stock price reaches its highest or lowest point.